GRAND
NEW
PARTY

Also by Ross Douthat

*Privilege: Harvard and the Education
of the Ruling Class*

GRAND NEW PARTY

How Republicans Can Win the Working Class
and Save the American Dream

Ross Douthat
and
Reihan Salam

DOUBLEDAY
New York London Toronto Sydney Auckland

DD

DOUBLEDAY

PUBLISHED BY DOUBLEDAY

Copyright © 2008 by Ross Douthat and Reihan Salam

All Rights Reserved

Published in the United States by Doubleday, an imprint of The Doubleday Publishing Group, a division of Random House, Inc., New York.
www.doubleday.com

DOUBLEDAY is a registered trademark and the DD colophon is a trademark of Random House, Inc.

Library of Congress Cataloging-in-Publication Data

Douthat, Ross Gregory, 1979–
Grand new party : how republicans can win the working class and save the American dream / Ross Douthat and Reihan Salam.
—1st ed.
p. cm.
Includes index.
1. Party affiliation—United States. 2. Republican Party (U.S. : 1854–) 3. Working class—United States—Political activity. 4. Voting—United States—History—20th century. 5. Political planning—United States. 6. Conservatism—United States. 7. Political parties—United States—History—20th century. 8. United States—Politics and government—History—20th century. I. Salam, Reihan. II. Title.
JK2271.D68 2008
324.2734—dc22
2008011071

ISBN 978-0-385-51943-4

PRINTED IN THE UNITED STATES OF AMERICA

1 3 5 7 9 10 8 6 4 2

First Edition

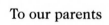

To our parents

CONTENTS

Contents

GRAND NEW PARTY

INTRODUCTION

American politics has awaited a new majority for nearly forty years. The old New Deal coalition began to crack up in 1968, inspiring regular talk about a permanent Republican realignment—in the Nixon era, the Reagan years, the Gingrich moment, and finally in the age of Bush. Yet a substantial majority of the kind that Franklin Roosevelt and Lyndon Baines Johnson enjoyed has persistently eluded the Republican Party. It wasn't until 2000, thirty-two years after Nixon first broke the Democrats' hold on power, that the GOP achieved control of the presidency and both branches of Congress, and then only by the barest of margins. Just six years later, a bollixed war and a record of domestic mismanagement cost them both houses, leaving the country more or less where it stood throughout the 1980s and 1990s—with a government persistently divided against itself.

This back-and-forth, in which the country tilts right but never quite delivers itself into the hands of the GOP, has frustrated liberals and conservatives alike. On the Right, it's produced a palpable sense that what should be their years in majority are being stolen from them—whether by the legacy of Watergate in the 1970s, gerrymandering in the 1980s, or the wiles of Bill Clinton in the 1990s. On the Left, the failure of conservatives to attain LBJ- or FDR-style majorities has bred a persistent delusion that the Democrats can be restored to power with minimal effort—by Jimmy Carter in 1976, perhaps, or by Bill Clinton and the New Democrats in 1992, or by the "emerging Democratic majority" that many left-wing pundits descried on the horizon at the turn of the millennium, only to have the advent of George W. Bush expose it as a mirage.

At the root of both sides' disappointment is the refusal of America's working class—the non–college-educated voters who make up roughly half of the American electorate, and whose parents and grandparents once formed the heart of the Roosevelt coalition—to pick a side and stick with it. Since 1968, these voters have provided the "silent majority" that elected Nixon, the "Reagan Democrats" who gave the Gipper his landslides, and the "angry white men" who put the Gingrich GOP over the top in 1994. They have transformed the Republican Party from the "party of the country club" to the "party of Sam's Club," in Minnesota governor Tim Pawlenty's memorable phrase. Yet after each Republican triumph, this working-class constituency—the Sam's Club voters, if you will—has become disillusioned with conservative governance and returned to the Democratic column: It happened with Carter, it happened with Clinton, and it happened again in 2006, after just four years of undivided Republican control.

Conservatives and liberals both have their preferred narratives of working-class politics since the 1960s, but neither adequately explains this unfinished realignment. In the Republican story, the working class didn't leave the Democratic Party; the party left them—by throwing in its lot with the worst excesses of the New Left, and embracing foreign-policy weakness, destructive cultural permissiveness, and a "war on poverty" that coddled deadbeats and criminals. At the same time, the demise of socialism demonstrated the moral and economic superiority of capitalism, and working-class voters began to vote their aspirations rather than their fears, rejecting the big-government condescension of American liberalism in favor of the empowerment that accompanies lower taxes and deregulation, weakened unions, and global free trade.

This story helps explain why working-class voters turned to the right from 1968 on, but it doesn't explain why they frequently slide back leftward, because its sunny free-market optimism glosses over the persistent unpopularity of the GOP's small-government message among the Sam's Club constituency. There have been moments when a "government is the problem" argument has resonated with working-class Americans, but for the most part, conservatives have conspicuously failed to earn their trust on most domestic policy questions. Even when non–college-educated Americans are pulling the lever for the GOP, they consistently give the Democratic Party higher marks on issues ranging from education to health care to Social Security, and two generations of conservative activists, authors, and politicians haven't been able to change their minds.

Yet they generally don't vote on these issues alone, and this is where the liberal narrative comes in. Yes, many liberals say, working-class Americans did part ways with the Democrats over issues like affirmative action and crime, national security and sexual permissiveness—but they did so only because the Republicans tricked them into thinking that those issues were more important than the litany of economic concerns that built the Roosevelt majority. Under Nixon, this argument runs, the Right played on white, blue-collar voters' basest instincts, convincing them that the Negro in their schools and on their streets was an existential threat that trumped their economic interests. Under Reagan and the elder Bush, it was the same old game, only this time played more subtly—using code words like "welfare queen" and "Willie Horton" to stir up racist feelings that most voters probably didn't even know they had. ("I remember looking at these people in the voting line," Bill Clinton recently remarked of the 1980 election, "and thinking, Oh my God, it's going to be a long night, because they were just glassy-eyed. They were there like somebody had fed them some sort of a controlled substance.")

Lately, as race has receded as a major national issue, the conservative con has supposedly grown more subtle still, relying on a wide array of culture-war controversies to keep the working class securely in its corner. In 2004, Thomas Frank, the most talented of the Left's cultural critics, limned this supposed deception in *What's the Matter with Kansas?*, his opus on working-class backlash. Today's Sam's Club voters are, according to Frank, voting on "cultural wedge issues like guns and abortion and the rest whose hallucinatory appeal would ordinarily be far overshadowed by material concerns." Conservative policies have immiserated the hardy Kansan laboring classes and fattened up the fat cats, but whereas once the farmers and laborers would have risen up to make the "bastards pay," today they're led rightward by conservative pied pipers, who conjure up a fictive Christmas-banning, gay-marrying liberal conspiracy to absorb the brunt of Middle American outrage.

This sorry state of affairs isn't just the fault of conservative con men and their GOP-voting dupes, Frank insisted; it's also the fault of the Democrats, whose cowardice on trade, taxes, unions, and other bread-and-butter questions of economic justice leave these Sam's Club voters with nothing else to vote *for*. The "third way" triangulation of the Clinton years, with its emphasis on the interests of the upper-middle class, was a "criminally stupid strategy" that took economic populism off the table and remade the Democrats as the "other pro-business party." With no one looking out for their economic interests, the poor buffeted plainsfolk of Kansas are pushed into the hands of a cynical GOP, which stokes culture-war outrage but never follows through: "Abortion is never halted. Affirmative action is never abolished. The culture industry is never forced to clean up its act."

The Frank thesis attracted an array of criticisms (not least for its aversion to detailed data), but it resonated with liberals nationwide, and after President Bush's reelection, the already successful book zoomed up the charts as the best, and indeed perhaps the only, explanation for why this manifestly unintelligent, unworldly, reckless, religious man won the votes of a majority of Americans. As a result, the 2006 election became the season of Thomas Frank. Though rarely invoked by name, the renewal of Democratic populism, particularly in the "Red states" so many liberals had written off, bore his stamp. Clinton's Third Way was dead, and in its place came candidates like Sherrod Brown of Ohio, railing against malefactors of great wealth and, in the new parlance of ex-Clintonites everywhere, "job-killing trade agreements." And as seats flipped across the country, no one must have been more pleased with the results than Frank himself. His thesis, after all, was vindicated.

Or was it? The Democrats recaptured both chambers of Congress in 2006, but by the barest of margins, and in a year when the GOP was buffeted by corruption and a mismanaged war. In specific cases—Brown in Ohio, James Webb in Virginia—a full-throated populism pushed a Democrat over the top, but on a national level, the GOP's losses had as much to do with Iraq, Katrina, and a series of damaging scandals as with the Democrats' sudden rediscovery of that old-time Roosevelt religion. Which means, in turn, that the hosannas that followed the Democratic victories of 2006 may prove just as premature as those that followed the 1974 anti-Nixon landslide, or Clinton's victory in 1992.

It's not that Frank-style populism can't win working-class

votes for the Democratic Party—it can. But it usually wins them only during economic downturns or eras of GOP misrule, and it hasn't kept Sam's Club voters in the Democratic column, or built a sustainable political majority, because its vision of American politics is largely false. Frank's central argument, in particular, is appealing but flat wrong: The poorest Americans *haven't* turned right over recent decades, under the influence of those "hallucinatory" culture war issues. Instead, they've turned left, voting for Democrats more reliably than even in the heyday of the Great Society. But this turn hasn't delivered liberals a majority, because most working-class voters aren't poor. They're relatively prosperous, in spite of left-wing claims about their supposed immiseration.

The problem for Frank and like-minded liberals is that they imagine the working class as it was sixty years ago—a mix of Joad-like farmers and unionized industrial workers, bound together by their antagonistic relationship to big business and dependent on redistributionist policies for their economic security. In reality, if you're a Sam's Club voter today, you're far more likely to be working in education or health care, office administration or business services than on a farm or an assembly line. You're more likely to belong to a family that makes $60,000 a year than one that makes $30,000. You probably own an array of electronics that would have dazzled your parents and grandparents; you enjoy cable TV, the high-speed Internet, and a car that puts the land yachts of the sixties to shame; and thanks to Wal-Mart and all its big-box peers, you spend less of your income on the necessities of life than any generation before you. (It's worth noting, too, that just about all of these advances can be attributed to the very same "job-killing trade agreements" so often described as the natural enemy of lower-income Americans.)

None of this means that the working class no longer exists, or that class politics no longer resonate. But it means that the working class of today is defined less by income or wealth than by education—by the lack of a college degree and the cultural capital associated with it. A diploma isn't a prerequisite for individual success: Many men and women in the Sam's Club demographic become quite comfortable, even rich, without graduating from college. But these individuals are the exception, and the larger non–college-educated demographic *is* enduring a slow-burning crisis, just as Frank argues, a crisis that has sent them ricocheting from Nixon to Carter to Reagan to Clinton to Bush in search of a politics that addresses their concerns. But it's not a crisis created by wicked plutocrats and their Republican enablers, and it's unlikely to be solved by stronger unions, more food stamps, a war on Wal-Mart, or the nationalization of a major industry or two. It's a crisis of insecurity and immobility, not poverty, and it's a crisis that has as much to do with culture as with economics.

The economic trends are important, certainly. Globalization and the rise of the knowledge-based economy, growing outsourcing and the demise of lifetime employment, the expansion of credit card debt, the decline of retirement and health-care security, the pressure from below created by unprecedented illegal immigration—all of these developments of the last three decades have made American workers feel more insecure, even though they're materially better off than ever before. And there's no question that the Republican Party has failed to adequately address these concerns, or that the GOP's emphasis on economic growth over economic security has made working-class life more unstable than it otherwise would have been.

But the "social issues," from abortion and marriage law to the death penalty and immigration, aren't just red herrings distracting the working class from their economic struggles, as liberals have insisted for the better part of forty years. Rather, they're at the *root* of working-class insecurity. Safe streets, successful marriages, cultural solidarity, and vibrant religious and civic institutions make working-class Americans more likely to be wealthy, healthy, and upwardly mobile. Public disorder, family disintegration, cultural fragmentation, and civic and religious disaffection, on the other hand, breed downward mobility and financial strain—which in turn breeds further social dislocation, in a vicious cycle that threatens to transform a working class into an underclass.

Sam's Club voters have been wobbling on the edge of this abyss ever since the social revolution of the sixties, which was a liberation for those equipped to deal with its freedoms but a slow-motion disaster for those Americans who lacked the resources and social capital to rebound from illegitimacy, broken homes, and failed marriages. Over the last thirty years, familial stability has gone from being a near-universal feature of American life to a privilege reserved for the mass upper class, whose wealth and education protect them from the disruptions that create divorce and single parenthood, and who have the social capital to pass these advantages on to the next generation. The result has been a persistently stratified America, in which working-class voters lack both personal and professional stability—and lack, as well, a way to rise in a country where success is increasingly tied to education, and education is tied to stable families, and both are out of reach.

Left unaddressed, these problems may only grow worse. The continued decline of the two-parent family means that more and more working-class Americans, white and Hispanic as well as black, will grow up without the kind of familial environment that's crucial to success in the information age. The combination of stagnating wages, the cost of supporting baby boomer retirees, rising gas prices, and a decaying, out-of-date transportation infrastructure will leave more and more young working families stuck in the high-priced megalopolises along the coast, as service-sector handmaidens to those fortunate enough to enjoy the benefits of what Michael Bloomberg has described, all too aptly, as the "luxury good" that is an upper-middle-class lifestyle in New York City. Continued mass immigration will exert downward pressure on wages for low-skilled workers, strain the government's ability to deliver needed social services, and exacerbate the cultural divide that's opened between the Sam's Club demographic and the mass upper class. And all of these problems have the potential to feed on another, breeding not only stagnation but downward mobility; not only inequality but permanent stratification; not only persistent poverty but rising crime; not only anti-immigrant anxieties but outright xenophobia; not only skepticism about the free market but populist fury.

Given these perils, where are Sam's Club voters to turn? The populist Left is responsive to their economic difficulties but allergic to moralism in public policy, and deeply resistant to any cultural critique of post-sixties America. Worse, its immediate wish list of economic "solutions"—increased spending on failing public schools, a more generous safety net for welfare recipients, amnesty and benefits for illegal aliens, the indefinite extension of race-based affirmative action programs, environmental regulations that kill jobs and drive up real estate prices—often seem designed to take money *out* of the pocket of the average Sam's Club voter. The moderate middle, meanwhile, is defined by its support for the status quo—free trade and cultural progressivism, secularism or a liberal religiosity, fiscal responsibility and continued large-scale immigration. These are the politics, allowing for certain variations, of Arnold Schwarzenegger and Joe Lieberman, Hillary Clinton and Colin Powell, the mass media and the business class. They aren't the worst set of ideas to dominate American politics, but they're inadequate to the challenges facing working-class America and the country as a whole.

Some combination of the populist Left and the neoliberal center is likely to emerge as America's next political majority even so, if the conservative movement can't find innovative ways to address the anxieties of working-class America. A Frank-style leftism, with its rage against corporations and its suspicion of free markets, is unlikely to sustain a long-term Democratic majority. But beneath the class-war rhetoric of the Webbs and the Browns, and the revival, in the current Congress, of a host of bad ideas from the 1970s, it's possible to glimpse a new liberal consensus taking shape, one with the potential to achieve the kind of realignment that Karl Rove and George W. Bush's GOP briefly had within its grasp. This new-model liberalism would wed the free-market centrism of the Clinton years to a revived push for European-style social democracy, the American Left's age-old dream. In theory, it would be committed to maintaining robust GDP growth and low unemployment, looking to relatively vibrant economies like Denmark as a model for American liberalism to follow. In practice, it would attempt to solve the problems of family breakdown and socioeconomic stratification by vastly expanding the tax-and-transfer state, with new bureaucracies, increased welfare spending, and rising public-sector employment smoothing over the anxieties of working-class life.

This is, in many respects, a deeply un-American solution to the problems facing our country, one that would emphasize dependence over self-sufficiency and bureaucratic condescension over self-help. But it's more of a solution than many Republicans seem prepared to offer. If liberal Democrats want to clientalize the common man, increasing his security at the expense of his independence, conservative Republicans often seem disinterested in his plight entirely, even when working-class votes are putting them over the top every November. The small-government movement deserves a great deal of credit for turning back the push for ever-larger bureaucracy and ever-greater federal power. But too many on the Right seem to have confused the American tradition of limited government for an ahistorical vision of a government that does nothing at all—that has no economic policy, for instance, save to stand back and let the gross domestic product rise and assume that every boat will rise along with it.

Having turned class politics to its advantage on cultural matters, by highlighting the gulf between Middle American values and the mores of the liberal overclass, the conservative movement has missed opportunity after opportunity to do the same on the economic front—by confusing being pro-market with being pro-business, by failing to distinguish between spending that fosters dependency and spending that fosters independence and upward mobility, and by shrinking from the admittedly difficult task of reforming the welfare state so that it serves the interests of the working class rather than the affluent. In the process, the Right has (thus far) squandered the chance to forge a conservative class consciousness among working-class voters, a unity of political allegiance and socioeconomic identity that, in its liberal form, made the Roosevelt coalition so potent and enduring.

Worse, conservatives have become confused about the legacy of the greatest conservative president of the modern era, Ronald Wilson Reagan. To hear today's conservatives tell it, Reagan was a man of unbending libertarian purity, whose domestic policy consisted of heroic tax cutting and little else. Cut taxes the Gipper surely did, but he was far more flexible and innovative in his pursuit of reform than his admirers—like the ten GOP presidential candidates who lined up to do him homage at the Reagan Library debate in 2007—would have you believe. Reagan was a president who cut income taxes dramatically but also closed corporate loopholes and raised taxes on gasoline; who slashed welfare spending but also midwifed the working poor–friendly Earned Income Tax Credit into being; who proposed reforming Social Security but also floated a plan for catastrophic health-care coverage; who attacked big government but also insisted, in his first inaugural, that his mission was not "to do away with government" but "to make it work—work with us, not over us; to stand by our side, not ride on our back."

This was the vision of modern conservatism—ideologically principled but politically pragmatic, interested in reforming the welfare state where it couldn't be abolished—that animated the Contract with America as well. And it was a vision that the Bush presidency attempted to restore, after the small-government movement ran aground in the late 1990s. But Bush's vision was long on rhetoric (the "investor class," the "ownership society," and of course "compassionate conservatism") and short on results; it attempted to ape liberal interest-group politics rather than forging a broader right-wing consensus among working- and middle-class voters; and its attempts to reform the welfare state were easily co-opted by self-interested operators—the Jack Abramoffs of the movement—who channeled Bush's reformist gestures into handouts for the Republican Party's business-class backers. If the Left sometimes seems to want to turn the United States into Europe by swaddling working-class voters in a cradle-to-the-grave welfare state, the Bush-era GOP's mix of neglect and crony capitalism too often appeared bent on pushing the United States toward Latin America—where the rich are rich, and the poor are poor, and there's no independent, self-sufficient working class in between.

The alternative to these two dangers is for America to continue to be, well, America—a nation of limited government and strong cultural solidarity, in which the goods of our national life are distributed as widely and equitably as possible, without sacrificing ownership and self-reliance in the process. Forty years after the dissolution of the old New Deal coalition, the United States needs leaders capable of articulating this distinctively American, distinctively democratic vision, and capable, too, of crafting a new majority to cope with the challenges it faces.

This is a book written for such a leader, and for anyone who believes that American politics should be oriented around the interests of the common man. We begin by describing the last successful attempt at such a politics—the New Deal of Franklin Roosevelt, which found the working class in difficulties similar to those it faces now, charted an ideologically innovative path out of the crisis, and (for all its faults) created an era of unprecedented political consensus, social equality, and cultural solidarity. In Chapters 2 through 5, we describe the breakdown of this consensus and the attempts by Republicans and Democrats alike to craft a new majority out of the wreckage of the Roosevelt Coalition. In Chapter 6, we consider the state of working-class life at the close of the Bush era, and the array of problems that a politics aimed at the interests of the common man would need to address.

Then, in the final three chapters, we attempt to sketch out a vision of what an ideologically innovative conservatism should actually be *for*, if it hopes to win working-class votes, craft a political majority, and redeem the promise of American life from the challenges it faces. A succession of presidents have groped toward this goal; a generation of intellectuals have proposed blueprints, feuded over details, or denied that any danger exists at all. But the country remains divided and the larger challenges endure unmet, waiting for a new generation wise enough to recognize the growing threat to the American Dream, and bold enough to do something about it.

PART I
THE UNFINISHED REALIGNMENT

1

The Old Consensus

When Barry Goldwater lost the 1964 presidential election by 16 million votes, carrying only six states and faring worse than any major-party candidate since Alf Landon in 1936, nobody seriously entertained the possibility that conservatism would rise from his defeat, let alone that the race might mark the beginning of a decades-long realignment in American politics. The Goldwater debacle was greeted instead as a welcome affirmation of a political and cultural order that had endured since the New Deal thirty years before. There had been intimations, in the early 1960s, that this consensus might be headed for a precipice, and so its custodians greeted the election results with head-nodding, hosannas, and more than a little relief. Like a man whose tumor has proven benign, they insisted vehemently that they had never doubted the happy outcome for a moment. Everywhere in autumn 1964 there were panegyrics to the center, to consensus, to the conventional wisdom—all of which conservatives had dared to challenge, and all of which had risen, as every pundit had always known they would, to cast Goldwater down to a devastating defeat.

This old and fated consensus called itself "liberal," and indeed it was, in the sense that Americans of the 1950s looked to government as the source of wealth and progress more than in any era before or since. They had every reason to—thanks to World War II and the Cold War, the federal government almost doubled in size between 1940 and 1960, and American prosperity rose with it. The critics of Franklin Delano Roosevelt fell silent, the long Republican presidency of Dwight Eisenhower accepted the innovations of his Democratic predecessors, and New Deal liberalism gave way to Cold War liberalism without skipping a beat or forfeiting its claim on the nation's loyalties. The American Right still threw up the occasional demagogue—a Douglas MacArthur, a Joseph McCarthy—and put liberals on the defensive, but neither the liberal coalition in politics nor the liberal dominance of the world of ideas seemed to face any serious challenge.

Yet the consensus of the 1950s was deeply conservative as well. It had been built by liberals, using liberal means, but it employed government power to preserve, rather than renovate, the most distinctive habits and institutions of American life. It wasn't just that the New Deal, for all its socialist tendencies, ultimately preserved free-market capitalism at a moment when many intellectuals were ready to abandon it. It was that the Roosevelt majority helped save the ideal of a self-sufficient working class, which had been central to American life from the beginning. And it did so by mixing economic liberalism with social conservatism, a potent political combination that raised America's working class, our democracy's natural political majority, to heights of security and self-confidence unseen before and since.

The Ownership Society

The interests of the working class—the common man, the hardworking but unexceptional citizen—have been at the heart of every great American political movement. From Jefferson to Lincoln to Roosevelt to Reagan, our most successful leaders have sought the democratization of wealth, competence, and social standing—not so that every American might be rich or famous, but so that we might all be independent and self-reliant and secure. In this sense, the American dream is ultimately a dream of home, of a place to call your own, earned and not inherited, and free from the petty tyrannies of landlords, bureaucrats, and bankers. It's a dream of a country in which ownership is available to everyone, provided that they are willing to work for it, rather than being handed out on the basis of wealth or caste, brains or beauty.

Both our political choices and our cultural habits have made the dream a reality. In the early republic, when land was the vehicle for ownership and independence, the federal government added nearly 2 million square miles to the original United States; it pursued policies, from the ordinances of the 1780s onward, to ensure that ownership would be as widely distributed as possible; and it invested in massive "internal improvements," from highways and canals to the transcontinental railroad, to make the settlement of the American interior possible. The same period that saw the violent rooting-out of the greatest internal challenge to America's ownership society—the slave economy of the South—also saw the passage of the Homestead Act, by Republicans who were nearly as exercised by "wage slavery" as they were by the real thing. The act was the defining government policy of America's agrarian era, in a sense—an attempt to preserve the openness and mobility of a society built around yeoman farmers and to prevent the emergence of a hidebound, class-ridden society built on the backs of industrial laborers.

The contrast with how Europe's governments treated the working class during the same period is instructive. Both continents extended the franchise, but Europe's nations did so out of fear: As British prime minister Earl Grey put it with admirable honesty in 1831, "The Principle of my reform is to prevent the necessity of revolution"—the nonmetaphorical kind of revolution in which elites get their heads chopped off. America, on the other hand, did so out of hope—the hope of attracting settlers, as states competed to offer the most expansive definition of political freedom, the better to lure enterprising pioneers. Similarly, Bismarck's Germany adopted the most ambitious program of social insurance in the world, the better to keep the factories running smoothly, but German elites were far less inclined to expand access to education. The goal was to create a docile working class, not an educated and ambitious one. America, in contrast, expanded schooling first and adopted social insurance programs only in the twentieth century. In each case, America's leaders wanted self-sufficiency and independence; Europe's wanted conformity and obedience.

But all the government interventions in the world wouldn't have succeeded without America's distinctive cultural habits. Politics provided the framework in which Americans pursued the dream of home, but culture provided the sense of solidarity and the moral guardrails necessary to sustain a society where the common man is independent of both state power and the dubious protections of noblesse oblige. The great danger of modern life is atomization and isolation, a danger that has prompted countless moderns to seek to impose order on their societies from above, either through totalizing ideologies—fascism and communism and all their variations; Salafist Islam—or the swaddling clothes of a nanny state. But America has avoided these temptations, relying instead on a powerful network of mediating institutions—churches and voluntary associations, marriage and family life—and an intense sense of national solidarity to provide a somewhat mysterious order from below.

"The central conservative truth," Daniel Moynihan famously remarked, "is that it is culture, not politics, that determines the success of a society." Being a liberal himself, he added that the "central liberal truth is that politics can change a culture and save it from itself." But the central *American* truth is that there's no way to cleanly separate politics from culture, or to separate either one from economics. Private virtue and cultural solidarity create economic security and independence; economic security enables people to persist in virtue; and wise public policy promotes both virtue and security at once. The reverse is also true—cultural dysfunction breeds economic dislocation and vice versa, while governmental folly can shape both culture and economics for the worse. And it has been the great achievement of American life that we have maintained, through many controversies, a healthy cycle rather than a widening gyre.

The Maternalist Moment

In the early years of the twentieth century, though, this achievement seemed in danger. The frontier had finally closed, and industrialization and urbanization appeared to pose nearly as great a threat as slavery to widespread ownership and equality-in-independence. The slave economy was regional and probably fated for extinction even without the Civil War; the industrial economy was national and insatiable. The laborer in the factory could never be as secure in his own home as the farmer with his own plot of land: The farmer controlled the means of production; the worker controlled only a piece of the assembly line. At its worst, industrialization seemed to betoken either a new era of wage-slave feudalism, or if you believed the Marxists, an end to the democratic dream and a merciless war of class against class.

America's reformers pursued a variety of responses to this crisis, all of them aimed at ensuring that labor replaced land as a vehicle for ownership and independence. High tariffs on

21

imported goods protected American manufacturers, and in theory provided them with the profit margins they needed to raise wages above subsistence level; immigration restrictions protected American labor from competition with foreign-born workers. Trusts were busted to break up cartels and keep the free market running smoothly, and labor laws instituted workplace protections and established an eight-hour day, effectively manufacturing scarcity to ensure that hourly wages went up. And unions gained ground, slowly but steadily, creating an economic climate in which the common man could bargain with the rich and claim his fair share of prosperity.

But one of the most important responses, and one of the least remembered, was the attempt to shore up family life, which seemed to be breaking down under the pressures of the new economy. The massive shift from the countryside to the cities, and the concurrent shift from large, extended families rooted in rural communities to small, unstable families dependent on wage work, wrested all but the wealthiest and most secure Americans from traditional sources of moral and economic support. Marriage rates fell, divorce rates rose, and crime climbed steadily between 1900 and the 1920s. Even though America was wealthier than Europe on a per capita basis, the infant mortality rate was twice as high in affluent America as it was across the Atlantic, and the rate of maternal deaths in childbirth was appallingly high. Some suspected that these shocking statistics could be attributed to immigration, but as the pioneering medical researcher Josephine Baker found in 1922, rates of infant mortality were in fact highest among the children of *native-* born American mothers.

For a small clique of highly educated women, which included pioneers in the social sciences and social work, these dispiriting numbers needed to be counted against all the technological marvels and therapeutic advances made possible by industrialization. These women, later dubbed the "maternalists," saw the slow, steady disintegration of the American family under radically new economic conditions as the central challenge of their time. They condemned Big Business's efforts to efface and undermine the value of domestic work as the entering wedge of a broader campaign to reduce self-reliant citizens to mere consumers and clients. In the words of Allan Carlson, the best recent historian of their movement, the maternalists "defined the family as the true crucible of Americanism, and held up the mother['s role] . . . as their economic and political program for renewal."

These arguments stood in opposition to the prevailing spirit of the age. The outsourcing of functions that had once belonged exclusively to the household was the source, after all, of America's industrial success. It seemed perfectly natural that this logic should extend from the manufacture of durable goods to the intimate sphere. As William Ogburn, a family scholar at the University of Chicago and an adviser to Herbert Hoover, memorably put it, the "barriers of custom" that kept women in the home simply meant that the "community is not making the most of this potential supply of able services." That was certainly the conclusion of the industrial barons who depended on the nimble hands of young mothers. The public schools, in the words of critic Florence Kelley, increasingly aimed "to prepare girls to become at the earliest moment *cash children* and *machine tenders*." At the same time, the National Association of Manufacturers joined with equity feminist groups like the National Women's Party in opposing legislation that would offer any special treatment to women in the workforce. And all of these forces coalesced around the then-dominant Republican Party, whose technocratic, pro-industry confidence would reach its peak in the Hoover years.

Against these trends, the maternalist thinkers—Jane Addams, Josephine Baker, Julia Lathrop, Florence Kelley, and Frances Kellor, among several others—devised a highly original ideological synthesis to address the threat that industrialization posed to the working class. Addams's famous Hull House defended the interests of women and children by attacking poverty's roots in social atomization, and the network of Settlement Houses that imitated Hull House's success were incubators for policy innovation on a national scale. Their founders pushed for child labor laws, for public schools that taught homemaking as well as bookkeeping, for campaigns to reduce infant and maternal mortality, and for symbolic statements like the establishment of Mother's Day. They tugged at the heartstrings of American voters, framing their cause as a simple matter of "baby-saving." As Lillian Wald, founder of the Henry Street Settlement, put it, "If the government can have a department to take such an interest in the cotton crop, why can't it have a bureau to look after the nation's child crop?"

By 1912, the federal government had established the U.S. Children's Bureau to do exactly that. Led by Lathrop, the Children's Bureau agitated from within the government for sweeping reforms designed to reduce infant mortality. Its greatest success was the Sheppard-Towner Act of 1921, which funded state-level programs in maternal and infant hygiene and a nationwide network of nurses and prenatal clinics. Like many of the New Deal programs it anticipated, the program was formally universal yet designed in such a way that working-class women reaped most of the benefits. Opposition from the American Medical Association eventually scuttled the act (then as now, the medical establishment seemed to fear the effects of democratizing access to medical knowledge), but only after thousands of maternity clinics were built across the nation and the nation's infant mortality rate had fallen dramatically.

Even more significant than the act itself, though, was the argument that Lathrop made on its behalf. Responding to critics who saw the legislation as somehow authoritarian or socialistic, she noted that the legislation sought "not to get the Government to do things for the family" but rather "to create a family that can do things for itself." With those words, Lathrop expressed a worldview that went on to inform, and sometimes even define, the New Deal.

The Conservative New Deal

The Great Depression threw the maternalists' concerns into sharp relief by revealing how vulnerable American families were to the fluctuations of the business cycle. Where the yeoman farmers of the early republic fell back on subsistence crops in times of crisis, the new urban families had access to cheap credit. This was a fair trade only until boom gave way to bust. Then the nightmare of dependency—on private charity, on the goodwill of a benevolent employer, or on the government dole—became a reality for even the most hardworking Americans. The confident Hoover technocrats who had urged Americans to accept the slow dissolution of the family for the sake of economic efficiency and progress were discredited for a generation, and the working class, who previously leaned Republican, turned to the Democratic Party in droves.

The New Deal, the fruit of this working-class realignment, offered a dubious hodgepodge of economic remedies, and its attempts at centralized planning and relentless scapegoating of business may have actually worsened the Depression. But the New Dealers' attempt at *social* reconstruction represented an impressive attempt to banish the nightmare of dependency for good, by tackling not only the economic crisis but its deeper cultural roots as well. To address the insecurity of working-class families, Franklin Roosevelt and his closest advisers sought to make capitalism safe for democracy, and vice versa, by opening a new frontier—this time a crabgrass frontier, spreading out from the smokestacks of the cities into what had been bucolic surroundings. Here wage earners would learn the dignity of

25

ownership and build their own communities beyond the supervision of the bosses. Here, workers could carve out what Christopher Lasch called a "haven in a heartless world," a space in which the family held pride of place.

At the core of this program was the push for the "family wage," an income standard that would enable a single breadwinner to support a homemaker wife and children. Almost every New Deal initiative sought to guarantee a family wage for male laborers, while limiting female employment or excluding women entirely. (The Works Progress Administration, for instance, allowed only one breadwinner per household to enroll, and held that a "woman with an employable husband is not eligible for referral as the husband is the logical head of the family.") Meanwhile, the New Deal's homeownership programs—the Home Owners' Loan Act of 1933 and the National Housing Act of 1934 chief among them—provided the impetus for an explosion of new construction in the suburbs, offering cheap mortgages that opened the crabgrass frontier to millions of working-class families.

A host of maternalists played a role in the New Deal, from Katharine Lenroot, who headed up the Children's Bureau from 1934 onward—the "primary essential of child welfare [is] a living wage for the father," she argued—to Mary Anderson, the head of the Labor Department's Women's Bureau, to Eleanor Roosevelt herself, who remarked that the "first ten years of a girl's marriage, broadly speaking, should be devoted to the home." But the central figure was Frances Perkins, the secretary of labor throughout FDR's time in office. Like her fellow maternalists, Perkins believed that industrialism had run rampant, invading what had been the more-or-less autonomous sphere of family life. Whereas the affluent could insulate themselves from this invasion, the poor could not. And so, drawing on the language of both social democracy and social conservatism, she made an egalitarian case for legislation that would protect this separate sphere. "The poor people have a right to their homes the same as the rich," Perkins insisted, "and we should not be allowed to enslave them to a form of industry which refuses them not only their liberty, but the wage which they ought to have in return for the labor they perform." Her rhetoric, which sounds antique to our ears, joined a critique of greed and corporate malfeasance to a forceful defense of traditional gender roles, a kind of left-conservatism that would define her most enduring achievement—Social Security.

In essence, the Social Security Act of 1935 aimed to meet the needs of what was then considered the "normal," and indeed the *normative*, family: a male head of household who served as the sole breadwinner, a mother who remained in the home, and three or more children. The program initially covered only the (largely male) population of industrial workers, and excluded professions like teaching and nursing. Women could claim benefits only if they were widowed, through the Aid to Dependent Children provision, which offered money to female-headed households in the hope of keeping widows out of the workforce. Later amendments made the program's social conservatism only more pronounced. Republicans made dramatic gains in the midterm congressional elections of 1938 in part by attacking Social Security for not spending enough, and the party pushed through measures—like a generous spousal benefit, which could be claimed *instead of* one's own benefits but not *in addition to* them—that actively incentivized women not to work at all, and excluded divorced women entirely. As Carlson puts it, the "1939 Amendments firmly established marriage, the 'family wage,' the stay-at-home mother, and the large family as the favored objects of public policy. Any deviation from these values—divorce, illegitimacy, working mothers, deliberate childlessness—faced financial disincentives."

Looking back from our postfeminist vantage point, it's easy to see this "family-centered welfare state," in Carlson's phrase, as little more than cover for sexism and the subordination of women—as, indeed, it often was. But it's also true that subordination comes in many forms. The maternalist side of the New Deal stifled the creativity and economic independence of women, no doubt, but the industrial transformation of American life had subordinated them in a different, potentially more devastating way, by devaluing domestic labor and threatening the economic independence of the family, the strongest bulwark against the imperialism of the industrial economy.

The maternalists—all of them highly educated and highly successful, not incidentally—saw this latter threat, the threat of wage slavery and the assembly line, as a greater danger to women than confinement to the domestic sphere, and acted accordingly. In an era before the birth control pill changed the interplay of biology and politics forever, it's hard to say that they were wrong, especially since their program ushered in nearly three decades of ever-increasing prosperity, security, and confidence for the American working class, women and men alike.

The Era of Good Feelings

"In the first decade of the twenty-first century," the libertarian writer Brink Lindsey remarked recently, "the rival ideologies of Left and Right are both pining for the '50s. The only difference is that liberals want to work there, while conservatives want to go home there."

Lindsey meant this as a criticism of Left and Right alike, but neither side's nostalgia is entirely misplaced. On the one hand, the period from 1945 to 1963 represented the high tide of government management of the economy—of large-scale unionization and progressive taxation, of widespread federal regulation and ever-expanding federal budgets, of CEOs who saw themselves as patriots first and profiteers second. At the same time, it was an era of profound social conservatism, in which the model of a male breadwinner, a female homemaker, and multiple children embodied the domestic aspirations of Americans from every walk of life.

The fruits of this dual consensus seemed to vindicate, almost completely, the maternalists' vision of how to build a thriving working class. The economic order reinforced the social order, and vice versa: There were stable families in every stratum of society, and rising incomes as well. Marriage rates soared, and birth rates followed; divorce rates plunged; the illegitimacy rate fell among rich and poor alike. The chaos associated with industrialization had been turned back, seemingly; civic life flourished, churchgoing rose, and crime rates fell and fell. Immigration had been tightly restricted, and assimilation had worked so well that fewer Americans spoke a foreign language in the fifties than at any point since the 1840s.

Duty, obligation, and personal responsibility were the watchwords of the era. The Hollywood heroes were strong, silent types like Gary Cooper and John Wayne, pop musicians sang about love and marriage instead of sex and violence, newspapers denounced divorce and covered up adulteries. The culture was more intellectual and more puritanical, and the two qualities were inseparable from one another. Today's liberals, feeling swamped by fundamentalism, pine for religious thinkers like Reinhold Niebuhr, but presumably not the Niebuhr who implied that Nelson Rockefeller's divorce and remarriage made him unfit for high office.

Everyone was confident, it seemed—in the federal government, in their churches and schools and police departments, in their scientists and professors and clergymen. And this confidence began at home. As Barbara Dafoe Whitehead would write, a generation later:

For the first time in history the vast majority of the nation's children could expect to live with married biological parents throughout childhood. Children might still suffer other forms of adversity—poverty, racial discrimination, lack of educational opportunity—but only a few would be deprived of the nurture and protection of a mother and a father. No longer did children have to be haunted by the classic fears vividly dramatized in folklore and fable—that their parents would die, that they would have to live with a stepparent and stepsiblings, or that they would be abandoned. These were the years when the nation confidently boarded up orphanages and closed foundling hospitals, certain that such institutions would never again be needed. In movie theaters across the country parents and children could watch the drama of parental separation and death in the great Disney classics, secure in the knowledge that such nightmare visions as the death of Bambi's mother and the wrenching separation of Dumbo from his mother were only make believe.

This unprecedented emotional security was matched and made possible by unprecedented economic security—and confidence, too, that better days were always ahead. Between the end of the Second World War and the beginning of the 1970s, American incomes doubled, and they doubled for *everyone*—dockworkers and druggists, secretaries and small businessmen. Vast fortunes became rarer even as the workingman's wealth increased. The economist Simon Kuznets's theory that income inequality would increase with industrialization and then begin to drop away toward zero—the famous "Kuznets Curve"—seemed vindicated: Inequality fell and fell, until the income distribution in the United States looked like a picket fence, with a roughly equal number of people in every segment.

Indeed, the very idea of a working class seemed outmoded,

given the kind of wealth that even the bluest-collar job could earn. As David Frum has noted, a man born in a tenement in 1920 where a single toilet served four families could go to work for the New York City Sanitation Department in 1945 and within five years afford "a semi-detached house in Bensonhurst with three bedrooms and a bath." He might not have refined manners or a college education, though he was confident that his kids or grandkids would, but he was a lot closer to the bourgeoisie than the Victorian proletariat. And in an age of cultural equality, when the rich drove almost the same cars as everyone else, ate roughly the same food, and watched exactly the same television shows, there seemed to be hardly anyone above him worth envying.

This was an illusion, in a sense, since working-class Americans weren't bourgeois in the nineteenth-century mode—they were employees, not employers; wage earners, not investors. As John Cassidy has written, "few inhabitants of California's Orange County or New York's Suffolk County owned factories or speculated on Wall Street. Most were regular employees of major corporations like McDonnell Douglas, Grumman or Hughes Aircraft. If they didn't go to work they risked losing their livelihoods, their houses and their cars. They were, in fact, not middle class at all in the Marxian sense of the word." But they were wealthy enough to *think* of themselves as middle class, a self-conception that endures to the present day.

And why shouldn't they? After all, the very idea of a class-conscious proletariat was, in some sense, un-American, a contradiction of the country's original democratic dream, in which differences in wealth were trumped by social equality. Industrialization had placed the dream in peril, but the efforts of the maternalists had brought the country safely through the storm, into a landscape where just as in the colonial era or the nineteenth-century West, every man could be his own master—or at least sit secure in a three-bedroom Bensonhurst home of his own.

Cracks in the Consensus

All these achievements, though, were built on a foundation of exclusion, and by the early 1960s cracks were beginning to show. For women, as we have seen, the maternalist valorization of the family required a workplace sexism that dramatically limited their aspirations, and long before the 1963 publication of Betty Friedan's *The Feminine Mystique*, this sexism began to chafe, as rising educational attainment led to a growing mismatch between women's skills and the horizons set by society. Meanwhile, the growing commercialism of 1950s America made the maternalist ideal of home economics, in which the domestic sphere played a productive rather than merely consumptive role, seem increasingly outdated. Labor-saving inventions left mothers with more time on their hands, and in place of the dignity of domestic labor that the maternalists had championed, as Carlson points out, the "image of the 'housewife' became a caricature, a woman dancing with her vacuum cleaner and pursuing 'the whiter than white' toilet bowl."

Among the elites who framed social policy, in particular, support for maternalism eroded, and it was abandoned in favor of a forthrightly emancipationist liberalism that focused on freeing individuals from the constraints of traditional family life rather than preparing them for its rigors. This was an understandable turn: The crisis of the 1920s and 1930s was long past, and the concerns of that era felt increasingly distant as well. It seemed like a propitious time to worry less about the interests of the working class—who had never been more prosperous, whose families had never been more stable—and more about the needs of others: the growing class of college-educated Americans, male and female alike, for whom the maternalist order felt increasingly like a "comfortable concentration camp," in Friedan's famous phrase; the atheists and anarchists, pornographers and misfits, rescued by an increasingly activist Supreme

Court from the postwar prison of censorship and enforced conformity; the "other America" languishing below the poverty line,
to whom the benefits of the era had failed to trickle down; and
even the huddled masses beyond America's borders, excluded
from the benefits of the golden age.

And, of course, African Americans. The maternalists, no rac-
ists themselves, hoped that the promotion of bourgeois norms
would guarantee the rapid assimilation of blacks into the increasingly prosperous mainstream of American life. In practice, though, the New Deal's program tended to exclude African
Americans from the benefits of the maternalist order, creating
an era, in Ira Katznelson's apt turn of phrase, "when affirmative action was white." Relief efforts were administered in ways
that favored whites, particularly in the South; new labor laws
excluded agricultural and domestic laborers, both heavily black
occupations at the time, from their regulations; so too, until
the 1950s, did Social Security. (Fully 65 percent of American
blacks were ineligible for Social Security in its 1935 incarnation.) The persistence of black poverty meant that while the
family-centered welfare state enabled *white* women to escape
the burdens of industrial labor, black women continued working
in large numbers—which may explain, in turn, why the black
family was the only area of society in fifties America where
divorce and illegitimacy were growing problems. Even the G.I.
Bill, perhaps the most successful social legislation in American
history, had the perverse effect of widening racial disparities.
Millions purchased new homes and acquired advanced degrees,
and black veterans were among them—but at far lower rates
than their white counterparts, in part because the administration of G.I. Bill programs was kept firmly in local hands. The result was the massive disparity in home ownership that persists
to the present day.

Over time, it became clear that the New Dealers had made
a deal with the devil to pass sweeping social legislation, refus-

ing to confront segregation head-on in the interests of keeping the South solidly in the Democratic column. Like the exclusion of women, the exclusion of blacks gradually sapped the old consensus's legitimacy, fueling a rising sense—among blacks, but also among white liberals—that there was something rotten with the liberalism of the maternalist New Deal. And it was precisely the astonishing prosperity of the 1950s that turned resentment and disquiet into open dissent: As white families rocketed to new heights of prosperity and black families lagged behind, racist exclusion bumped up against rising expectations, and racial tension was the inevitable result.

Finally, there was growing resentment against government itself. The old consensus worked for the working class, but it was a wartime consensus extended to peacetime, and it inevitably began to chafe. The "family wage" regime worked, but only so long as Big Business, Big Government, and Big Labor were hand in glove, and the individual's economic and political freedoms were stifled to a degree unimaginable before or since. If you ran General Motors or worked for it, there had arguably never been a better time to be an American. But if you were a small businessman or an avant-garde artist, if you didn't like your union boss or didn't want to get drafted to go to Korea or Vietnam, if your old neighborhood stood in the way of your city's big redevelopment plan or you wanted to start an airline to compete with Pan Am—well, then maybe the golden age wasn't so golden after all.

The fifties consensus represented the end of ideology, according to Daniel Bell, which was true enough as far as it went. But America was still filled with ideologues and dreamers, left and right and somewhere in between, who were enduring the era of good feelings with thinly concealed distaste, waiting for the cracks to spread and the temple to come crashing down.

The Goldwater Moment

Such discontents made Barry Goldwater's candidacy possible; the energy of a rising generation of conservative activists made it inevitable. Nineteen sixty-four was the moment when the American Right came alive as a populist movement—as a revolt of businessmen against taxation, unions, and bureaucracy; anti-Communists against the accommodationist center and pinko Left; and Southerners against desegregation. None of these were new forces in American life: Right-wingers had been complaining about a sellout to Communism since Yalta; the civil rights battles had been raging since *Brown v. Board of Education*; businessmen had been griping about the size and scope of New Deal government since FDR's first term. But this was the first time the various discontents began to weave into something approaching a coherent ideology, a conservatism that amounted to more than "a series of irritable mental gestures," in Lionel Trilling's famous phrase. And something new was woven in as well—a sense that America's problems ran deeper than the intertwined menaces of Communism and big government, and that the new direction liberalism was taking, away from maternalism toward social engineering on the one hand and personal liberation on the other, might threaten not only individual liberty, but public morals and the social fabric as well.

Thanks to the gauzy nostalgia that liberals often cultivate toward a previous generation's conservative icons—the better to contrast the old, "honorable" right-wingers with their degenerate modern heirs—Barry Goldwater is remembered as a libertarian purist, a small-government crusader but also a foe of all moralists, and the rise of the Religious Right is remembered as a betrayal of his tolerant, laissez-faire vision. This may be an accurate description of the late-in-life Goldwater, who declared his support for gay rights and abortion-on-demand. But it was the senator from Arizona who actually pioneered the theme of moral decline, and the need for moral renewal, that has run through every subsequent conservative campaign.

It was Goldwater, in his convention acceptance speech, who warned of a "virtual despair among the many who look beyond material success for the inner meaning of their lives." It was Goldwater who declared that the "moral fiber of the American people is beset by rot and decay," Goldwater who called for the reinstitution of school prayer ("Is this the time in our nation's history for our Federal Government to ban Almighty God from our classrooms?" he asked), Goldwater who attacked the spread of pornography and praised "traditional values," Goldwater who used explicitly moral language to talk about crime and social disorder. These were, Rick Perlstein wrote in *Before the Storm*, his brilliant history of the 1964 campaign, a "set of lines that were new to conservative campaigning—and they were catching fire."

But not quickly enough to save Goldwater's candidacy. America in the early 1960s was on the cusp of a social revolution, and there were harbingers of unrest everywhere you looked— the sudden rise in crime, the uptick in divorce rates, the Supreme Court's school prayer decision, the protests at Berkeley, and the screaming girls at the Beatles' concerts. Timothy Leary, dismissed from Harvard, had just published *The Psychedelic Experience*; the Second Vatican Council met in Rome; the birth control pill flew off pharmacy shelves; *Playboy*'s cultural cachet was rising. But these were only harbingers, not upheaval itself, and it still seemed possible—no, likely—that the difficulties of the moment would quickly give way to the broad sunlit uplands of a New Frontier or a Great Society, and that the remarkable material and moral progress that had defined American life since Roosevelt still had decades left to run.

So working-class Americans toyed with Goldwater, nodded along to some of his speeches and worried over the direction of the country, but ultimately pulled the lever for the Democrats, as they had in every race for thirty years. When you polled blue-collar voters at the factory gates during the long hot summer of '64—the first of many such summers that decade—they leaned toward the Republicans; when November came around, they pulled the lever for Johnson, as did many GOP moderates and independents, who abandoned their ancestral party in a temporary flight that anticipated their more permanent shift into the Democratic column in the 1990s. Only the South responded to Goldwater, and even there it was only the Deep South, the diehard segregationist states, which swung GOP for the first time since Reconstruction. The better-off, rapidly modernizing Peripheral South still went for LBJ; it would turn to the Republicans only once the Democrats' assault on segregation gave way to a push for school busing and racial preferences, and the language of civil liberties seemed to become a shield for lawbreakers.

But that was all in the future. The Arizona senator had carried his movement within sight of the mountaintop, but neither he nor any other conservative—save perhaps a certain ex-actor from California—sensed a way to scale it and transform their angry minority into a governing majority. Up to a point, the Right of 1964 resembled the conservative coalition of the present day: There were the small businessmen, the government-cutters, the states'-rights Southerners, the evangelical preachers, and even the ex-Communist intellectuals—the *National Review* brain trust, whose political trajectory anticipated the neoconservative turn of the following decade. But the movement was a microcosm of a potential majority, not the real thing, and for all their biases and blindnesses, the pundits were correct—the Right of 1964 was too extreme to win working-class votes and thus elections, and too extreme to govern if it did.

The Right's intellectuals were brilliant, for instance, but many of them were also cranky Manichaeans, proudly out of step with their country's assumptions and aspirations. There were exceptions—William F. Buckley, Jr., of course, and the pragmatic William Rusher, who would do so much to build the majority to come—but for the most part the right-wing thinkers of the 1950s and early '60s were only half at home in modern America and prone to sweeping, implausible claims about the collectivist tyranny of the modern welfare state, and the inevitable decline of the West. Richard Weaver's nostalgia for the Old Confederacy; James Burnham's announcement of the West's suicide; Whittaker Chambers's remark that in abandoning Communism he had joined the losing side of history; Frank Meyer's casual reference to the "totalitarian implications of the federal school lunch program"—there was philosophical subtlety here, but it wasn't likely to resonate in a nation enjoying an unprecedented economic expansion, and basking in the noonday light of the first American century. Karl Hess was a more interesting mind than Theodore Sorensen, but Sorensen made the myth of Camelot sing for a generation, whereas Hess suggested that Goldwater tell the nation that extremism in the defense of liberty was no vice—which was perhaps true, but also perhaps not the wisest way to phrase it.

What was true of the intellectuals was likewise true of the movement as a whole. Time has vindicated the Right's opposition to Communism, at home and abroad, but it hasn't vindicated many of the particular causes that exercised conservatives in the 1950s—their willingness to defend and even honor Joseph McCarthy (a willingness that extended, embarrassingly, to Buckley himself); their obsession with the question of who had "lost" China to the Reds; their conviction that rollback, not containment, was the wisest way to confront and overcome the Soviet Union. The truer the believer, the more perfervid the anti-Communist fantasies, from John Bircher suspicions of Eisenhower's loyalties, to Phyllis Schlafly's dire warnings, in *A Choice Not an Echo*, about the "secret kingmakers in New York" bent on "perpetuating the Red empire in order to perpetrate the high level of Federal spending and control."

Worse, conservatives were wrong, sometimes honorably but often not, on the most pressing moral issue of the early 1960s—the civil rights movement. Liberals have used this failure to tar the Right as racist for over forty years, insisting that every conservative project—welfare reform, crackdowns on crime and drugs and disorder, opposition to affirmative action, support for federalism—*must* be motivated by the same atavistic hatreds that released attack dogs and bombed churches. The racist smear is one of liberalism's most wearying rhetorical tropes, but it wouldn't exist if conservatives had made different choices in the early 1960s and heeded the better angels of their nature.

Sometimes they were obtuse, as Goldwater was; no racist, he agonized over his vote on the Civil Rights Act, and ultimately decided to stand on federalist principle in a matter where that principle ought to have been compromised. Sometimes they were deceived by their own pleasant illusions, like the editors of *National Review*, who persisted in a nostalgic "white-man's-burden" fantasy, declaring in 1960 that "leadership in the South . . . quite properly rests in White hands," and adding with the pedantry of the entirely deluded that "upon the White population this fact imposes moral obligations of paternalism, patience, protection, devotion, and sacrifice." And sometimes—well, sometimes they were just plain racist.

Eventually, the Right would shake off this shameful legacy; eventually, too, conservatism would find leaders and intellectuals who would move the party into the American center that would soon be vacated by a self-destructing Democratic Party and who could move that center to the right as well, until on welfare and crime, taxes and moral values, the GOP was no longer sniping from the wilderness, but speaking for a national majority. But one great problem would linger, from that era until this one: the problem of government—its size, its goals, its obligations. If the conservatism of the early 1960s knew one thing, it was that the government was doing too much, spending too much, interfering with personal freedom too often and too broadly. If conservatives had one golden dream, it was not merely to slow government's growth, but to shrink it dramatically—to abolish cabinet agencies and vast, money-wasting programs, to return power to the states and tax dollars to the people. And if there was one aspect of conservatism that doomed Goldwater, it was precisely this desire to remake or do away with aspects of American government that working-class Americans understood as central to their prosperity.

Over the forty years since, this problem—that the working class wants, and needs, more from public policy than simply to be left alone—has prevented the Republican Party from consolidating an enduring majority, despite all the right-wing intellectual victories and all the conservative electoral gains. It defeated Goldwater, it stymied Reagan, it ruined Gingrich, and it crippled the domestic policy of George W. Bush. It was at the heart of a marginal conservatism's 1964 defeat, and it lies at the heart of conservatism's present crisis. Conservatives must either find a way to solve this dilemma or retreat into the political wilderness from whence they came.

2

The Crack-up

Somewhere between the assassination of John F. Kennedy and the election of Richard Nixon, America entered a period of crisis whose shadow still touches our national life. For a brief moment in the early 1970s, amid presidential malfeasance, revolutionary violence, and right-wing backlash, this crisis seemed almost existential, as though the United States might go the way of Weimar Germany or a failed Latin American republic. But that danger passed relatively quickly: By 1975, Watergate and Vietnam were in the rearview mirror, the Weathermen were in hiding and Patty Hearst was standing trial, George Wallace was in a wheelchair, and Kent State and the summer riots belonged largely to the past. Our political institutions tottered, but they righted themselves and have not been threatened since.

The crisis in working-class life, however, endured; indeed, it endures to the present day. "The Sixties," an inexact term for a period of change and chaos that extended well into the 1970s, posed four great challenges to the American working class, and particularly to those aspects of the American Dream—economic independence and cultural solidarity—that the New Deal had done so much to strengthen. There was the challenge to public order, embodied in the skyrocketing crime rate and the air of lawlessness that settled over the nation's cities; the challenge of family breakdown, visible in rising rates of illegitimacy, teen pregnancy, venereal disease, and divorce; the challenge of economic stagnation and then stratification, as working-class wages stopped rising and inequality began to grow for the first time in two generations; and finally a broader challenge to the country's cultural solidarity, driven by the emergence of a meritocratic elite at odds with the citizens they were supposedly charged with governing.

Each of these trends fed the others, like diseases battening on a weakened immune system, until untangling the various pathogens came to seem impossible. Worse, the liberal governing class, the heirs of the New Deal and the working-class majority it built, seemed helpless to do anything about the situation, and often denied that any crisis existed at all. This led, inexorably, to the breakdown of the Roosevelt coalition, and the beginning of the Republican realignment. The New Deal and a long peacetime economic expansion built the era of consensus; crime, contraception, and growing economic inequality tore it apart—and quickly.

Safety First

When Barry Goldwater ran for president on law-and-order themes and lost, the thirty-year crime wave that would dominate American political life until the mid-1990s was already under way, though nobody quite realized it yet. The middle decade of the twentieth century was probably the safest ten years in American history. In the 1940s and 1950s, the homicide rate steadily dropped, reaching a low of 4.7 murders per 100,000 Americans in 1957. In 1960, there were 60 reported robberies for every 100,000 people, 508 burglaries, 183 auto thefts, and just under 10 rapes. In a nation of 180 million people, only 288,000 violent crimes were reported. America's lawless past seemed to belong to a closed chapter of the nation's history.

But the golden age wouldn't last. By 1966, the murder rate had climbed to 5.6 per 100,000, even though the economy was still booming and the Great Society was on the march. In 1970, there were 7.9 homicides per 100,000; in 1975, 9.6; in 1980, 10.2. The rate of all serious crimes—which included robbery, rape, and assault as well as homicide—rose even faster, nearly tripling between 1960 and 1980. In that year, for every 100,000 Americans, there were 250 reported robberies (a fivefold increase), 1,684 burglaries (up threefold), 37 reported rapes (up fourfold), and 500 auto thefts (more than double). There were 225 million Americans in 1980, and over 13 million reported crimes. In the 1950s, crime happened to strangers; in the 1970s and 1980s, it happened to people like you.

"Root causes" were the midcentury consensus's big idea about lawbreaking, when the peaceable kingdom that America had become seemed to demonstrate that rising prosperity and growing equality, not enforcement and imprisonment, were the keys to cutting crime. And sure enough, there were many root causes that fed the explosion in crime rates—black outrage, finally bubbling to the surface after a hundred years of discrimination; the rise of the drug culture; the sheer size of the baby-boom generation, an enormous cohort of males entering adolescence all at once; and the regression to the moral mean that inevitably followed on the heels of the New Deal's attempt at Victorian remoralization.

This was the big picture, much of it beyond the control of any cop or congressman. But America's voters, and particularly its working-class voters, could be forgiven if they fixated on the most immediate factor in the epidemic, and the factor that seemed amenable to alteration—that crime was rising because it wasn't being punished. The sociologists of the 1950s had redefined criminality as a pathology, tied to race or class, that demanded a cure rather than incarceration, and the criminal justice system went along with them. In the 1960s, as David Frum has pointed out, while crime rates doubled and the overall population rose, the total number of incarcerated lawbreakers actually fell—from 212,953 inmates in 1960 to 196,429 a decade later. After the wartime siege mentality of the forties and fifties, it was inevitable that the legal pendulum would swing toward civil liberties, but not that the Supreme Court would do so much to undercut law enforcement—overturning laws against loitering and vagrancy, restricting searches and seizures, imposing harsh strictures on interrogations. Between 1960 and 1965, the Warren Court heard seventy-five cases in which criminals claimed that the police had violated their civil rights and found for the criminals in sixty-four of them. The cops got the message and acted accordingly: Spooked by fears of corruption and lawsuits, they sealed themselves off from the people they were supposed to protect. As William Tucker has pointed out, by the 1980s, "in some cities, patrol officers were not allowed to talk casually with civilians. In New York City, beat officers could not confront street corner drug dealers but had to buck the matter up to special units. As ordinary patrol cars continually drove by congregations of drug dealers without taking any note, neighbors became convinced that the police were corrupt and in the pay of the drug dealers."

The death penalty, likewise, was all but abandoned. Only three Americans were executed between 1965 and 1979, and a Supreme Court decision—*Furman v. Georgia*, in 1972—invalidated (temporarily) the death penalty statutes of nearly every state as "cruel and unusual." Again, it was a matter of mid-century confidence gone astray: In the early 1960s, reformers pointed out that execution was nearly always an extreme form of punishment, because 90 percent of murders were crimes of passion rather than cold-blooded killings. It was true enough at the time, but after two decades of a near-moratorium on capital punishment, nearly half of all murders were "stranger killings," often carried out to silence witnesses to other crimes. In the 1990s, predictably, the states that had reinstated the death penalty enjoyed the largest drop in their murder rates.

Inevitably, the working class bore the brunt of this rising violence. Many of its members had moved out to suburbs, but many more still lived in the increasingly chaotic cities, in the row houses and apartment buildings their "family wages" had purchased—in New York City, where the robbery rate rose fifteen-fold between 1965 and 1980; in Washington, D.C., where there were 81 murders in 1960 and 472 in 1990. They were the ones who sent their kids to public schools, where a 1979 study found that one out of every twenty teachers reported being the victim of an assault by a student. They were the ones asked to be guinea pigs in disastrous attempts at social engineering like the Boston busing project. The judge who authored the busing decision, naturally, lived in Cambridge and sent his kids to private schools.

So what did the working class do? They bought guns: American gun ownership rose from 30 percent to 40 percent between 1959 and 1973, and NRA membership tripled. They lost their confidence in the courts, in the cops, in the Congress; public confidence in American institutions plummeted in the late 1960s. They moved to the suburbs, though rising crime rates followed them there; indeed, suburban violent crime rates increased three times faster than urban violent crime rates in the 1970s, and rural crime rates crept upward as well, until by 1991, the crime rate in rural America was higher than the 1966 crime rate for urban America. And they started voting Republican—pulling the lever first for Nixon, and then, in greater numbers still, for Ronald Reagan.

Meanwhile, liberals consoled themselves with the knowledge that their old constituents' rightward turn was all about race.

Once LBJ associated the Democratic Party with the civil rights movement and racial equality, this argument runs, the Democrats effectively traded their racist constituents for the black vote and doomed their majority by the trade-off. Liberal righteousness on race enabled the GOP to tap into the racial resentments of Southern whites and working-class voters in the North and turn antiblack backlash to their advantage.

For liberals, this is the original sin of the American Right, the strategy whereby a generation of conservatives sold their souls and won their majority in a devil's bargain. And as with any powerful myth, it contains significant elements of truth. There's no question that from 1964 on, conservative Republicans abandoned any serious attempt to court the black vote and staked out an identity as the party that opposed the agenda of the civil rights movement; or that many racist voters switched from the Democratic to the Republican column after the 1960s; or that conservatives became adept at using various forms of symbolism to appeal to the prejudices of white Southerners (with the inevitable pilgrimages to Bob Jones University being obvious, and particularly egregious, examples).

But conservatives employed racist symbolism in certain locales and situations precisely because they were unwilling to promote racist *policies*—because they had abandoned their support for racial segregation and accepted the civil rights settlement of 1964 that Barry Goldwater had once opposed. In the liberal story line, this shift earns the Right no credit, because conservatives were still using issues like crime and public order to play on voters' deep-seated segregationist impulses. But there's little evidence that those impulses translated into votes outside the deepest South, or that opposition to the civil rights movement would have been a winning national issue for the GOP absent the crime wave and the subsequent association of the civil rights lobby with a blame-the-cops-first attitude toward lawbreaking.

Working-class Americans had their chance to vote their racist impulses in 1964, when Goldwater ran as the candidate of segregation and Johnson as the candidate of integration, and instead they helped deliver the Democrats the largest landslide in the party's history. The GOP traded the black vote for the ex-Confederate vote that year, and it was a net *loss* for the party—because outside Alabama, Mississippi, and the rest of the Deep South, it's worth remembering, the civil rights movement was extremely popular. In 1964, 70 percent of Americans supported the Civil Rights Act, a number that helps to explain why Johnson won 56 percent of the vote in segregationist North Carolina, 55 percent in segregationist Tennessee, and 56 percent in segregationist Arkansas, while keeping Northeastern and Midwestern blue-collar voters securely in his party's pocket as well.

The Border South and the white working class moved to the GOP column, eventually, but it wasn't the Civil Rights Act that did it; it was everything that happened next. There were racial resentments at work, certainly; opposing segregation was easier than accepting forced integration or affirmative action, and the principle of equality was easier to accept than the government-enforced practice of it. But what mattered most was the explosion in murder, rape, robbery, and vandalism rates and the failure of the governing class to perform the most basic task of government and keep its citizens safe from violence. Liberals didn't lose working-class votes because they were too noble—because desegregation, the "historic task the Democrats took on for the country," as Democratic pollster Stanley Greenberg put it recently in a representative liberal analysis of the era, consigned them to the political wilderness. They lost their majority, and deservedly so, because in an era of mounting lawlessness—violent crime went up *367 percent* between 1960 and 1980—they were unable to address widespread voter anxiety over the collapse of public order.

Yet a generation of potted histories have insisted there was something wildly ignoble about running campaigns, as Nixon's GOP did, on themes of "law and order" (inevitably placed in scare-quotes), and something bigoted and narrow-minded about voters who cast their ballots with such basic concerns in mind. In *Chain Reaction*, otherwise one of the smartest left-of-center books about the working class's rightward turn, Thomas and Mary Edsall remark that "crime became a shorthand signal, to crucial numbers of white voters, of broader issues of social disorder, tapping powerful ideas about authority, status, morality, self-control, and race"—as though it weren't more likely that crime itself *was* the issue, in an era of unprecedented lawlessness, and that all those "powerful ideas" were really just "shorthand signals" themselves, for voter anxiety over the safety of homes and neighborhoods. Or again, Greenberg's recent account of the period suggests that Nixon "fanned the flames" and "kept the country focused on disorder" (as if the country wouldn't have been fixated on it already!). "The Republicans' strategy," he complains, "was not to offer an alternative vision," but merely to campaign "for 'law and order'. . . amid the mounting disorder."

Merely to campaign for "law and order." This is history written from the vantage point of privilege, and it reflects, in microcosm, the problem that has dogged American liberalism ever since the 1960s: the divergence between the interests of its elite, well-heeled vanguard—in the case of crime and race, their interest in their own moral vanity—and the interests of the working-class voters who used to be the Democratic Party's base. The same pattern played itself out on issue after issue: Liberalism vacated the mainstream, and the Republican Party rushed (or stumbled, in some cases) into the breach.

The Personal Is Political

As with crime, so with sex. "Sexual intercourse began," the famous Philip Larkin rhyme runs, "In nineteen sixty-three /

(Which was rather late for me) / Between the end of the *Chatterley* ban / And the Beatles' first LP." Larkin was a poet, and so he can be forgiven for prioritizing culture, but though he gets the date roughly right, it was science, not D. H. Lawrence or the mop-tops, that created the modern era of sexual relations. Forget Elvis's hips, or Hefner's pinups, or *The Feminine Mystique*: It was orthotrycycline that changed America's sex life forever.

Prior to the advent of the Pill, both cultural mores and government policy emphasized the *differences* between men and women—the biological fact of childbearing and the sociological realities that flowed from it. Women bore children and men didn't, therefore men needed to be constrained into fulfilling their duties as fathers, therefore promiscuity and illegitimacy and divorce and adultery needed to be stigmatized. Women bore children and men didn't, therefore women were more vulnerable during sex than men, therefore sex needed to be treated as something significant or even sacred, and anything that threatened this approach—pornography, for instance, or contraception or even coed living arrangements—needed to be restricted or avoided at all costs. Women bore children and men didn't, therefore women were responsible for the domestic sphere, therefore the economy needed to *allow* them to be responsible for it, by paying male workers a wage sufficient to support their families while their wives remained at home.

This maternalist order was both protective and oppressive. It set familial stability as its highest value, which saved women from abandonment but also prevented them from leaving loveless or abusive marriages. It extolled a distinctively feminine approach to sexuality, in which romance was more important than sexual gratification, and the male impulse toward promiscuity was straitjacketed by monogamy—but as a result, it often dismissed the possibility of female sexual gratification outright, while treating "sluts" who deviated from the virtuous path far more harshly than it did "rakes" or "cads" who did the same.

It sheltered women from the burdens and miseries of the industrial economy, but it did so by condescending to them, by dismissing their own entrepreneurial instincts and throwing up obstacles to their participation in the workforce, and by maintaining a male stranglehold on economic and political power.

Given these trade-offs and cruelties, it's understandable that so many people, male and female, seized on the possibilities offered by the Pill—the possibility of a world in which men and women were essentially the same, equally liberated from the burdens of childbearing, equally free to participate in the workforce and thrive there, and equally capable of enjoying sex without worrying too much about the consequences. From unisex dormitories to unisex fashions, this dream of male-female sameness dominated the twenty years that followed. Labor force participation rates for women, at just 35 percent in 1950, jumped to 70 percent by 1980, as the notion of the "family wage" was abandoned (often to the relief of the companies that had been forced to pay it). In 1975, the Supreme Court ruled that Social Security could no longer pay survivors' benefits to widows but not widowers, rejecting the maternalist assumption that "women as a group would choose to forgo work to care for children while men would not."

Restrictions on condoms and pornography fell away; there was no-fault divorce in every state by 1985; cohabitation spread rapidly; and discrimination against unmarried couples was banned in many states. In 1977, the Supreme Court struck down laws that distinguished between the offspring of married and unmarried parents: The state, the justices confidently declared in *Trimble v. Gordon*, could not justify discrimination out of a desire to "promote legitimate family relationships." Then there was *Roe v. Wade*—the ultimate attempt, arguably, to liberate women from the demands of childrearing and to give them the same kind of freedom from sexual care enjoyed by men.

Convinced that men and women were different, the New Deal maternalists had sought to use government power to protect the domestic sphere from capitalism. Convinced that men and women were the same, the sixties-era feminists set out to use government power to make capitalism safe for women. Thus affirmative action and Title IX, thus the push to close the "pay gap" and smash the "glass ceiling," thus the demand that the government subsidize contraception and abortion. Thus the celebration of work as the ultimate form of self-actualization, and home life as a kind of wage slavery without the wages, in an exact reversal of the old maternalist take. Thus, too, the push for the Equal Rights Amendment, the high-water mark of birth-control-pill politics, which sought to enshrine the interchangeability of the sexes in the U.S. Constitution.

For a brief time, it seemed like the whole world could win. Women could finally be men's equals in the workplace and the bedroom; in return, men would be free to express *their* essential natures as sexual beings, freed from the constraints of lifelong monogamy. It would be the age of the *Playboy* man, loosed from the restraints of "Puritanism" that Hugh Hefner was always railing against; the age of the "sensitive man," the Alan Aldas and James Taylors, no longer stuck playing the strong silent breadwinner and free to get in touch with their feelings at last; the age of the liberated divorcée and the open marriage. Children would be happier: Birth control would make illegitimacy disappear, every child would be a wanted child, and even divorce, if handled correctly, would be a boon for the kids as well. ("Only by treating yourself as the most important person and not always sacrificing yourself for your children," the self-help guru Wayne Dyer explained in 1976's best-selling *Your Erroneous Zones*, "will you teach them to have their own self-confidence and believe in themselves.") Similar benefits would flow from legalized abortion: "We are impressed," declared the Rockefeller Commission Report on Population, convened by Richard Nixon in 1972, that the "availability of abortion on request causes a reduction in the number of illegal abortions, maternal and infant deaths, and out-of-wedlock births, thereby greatly improving the health of women and children." The American economy, too, would benefit from the new unisex world, by finally taking advantage of William Ogburn's "potential supply of able services" heretofore locked away in domestic life. Even the Earth would be better off: Population growth would be restrained, and the environment saved from the ravages of too many human beings.

Some of these hopes were ridiculous—the mid-seventies confidence that divorce would be good for the kids looks particularly lunatic in hindsight—but not all of them. For many Americans, particularly the better-off and better educated, quite a few of the Sexual Revolution's promises have been fulfilled, which explains why its achievements are so hotly defended in today's culture wars. But the difficulty is that the brave new world of oral contraceptives and androgyny, so egalitarian in theory, quickly began stratifying America as never before. As the old moral guardrails were stripped away, those Americans who had other guardrails to fall back on—wealth, education, good looks—thrived; those who didn't suffered. The new sexual free market was meritocratic rather than democratic; it favored the beautiful and the intelligent and the rich, while deliberately undercutting the institution that had traditionally provided the common man with stability and social capital: the two-parent family.

Yet just as they convinced themselves that the working-class backlash against crime was really about race, liberals explained the working-class backlash against the sexual revolution as a simple matter of cultural traditionalists (read: bigots) freaking out over uppity women, cohabiting kids, and secularization. Of course the working class objected to the new freedoms of the Sexual Revolution, this argument ran, because they were more religious and socially conservative (read: more ignorant) than their better-educated peers, and thus were easily offended by the brave new age of *Deep Throat,* abortion on demand, and women in the workplace. It wasn't liberalism's fault; blue-collar voters were just behind the times, and patience, education, and enlightenment would bring them back into the Democratic fold.

This account, like the racial theory of working-class realignment, is true up to a point—the working class was more culturally traditional, more religious, and yes, more bigoted in certain ways—but misses the larger picture. Working-class social conservatism, and the turn to the GOP it inspired, wasn't just the residue of ancestral prejudices; it was, and is, a rational response to lives lived without the security provided by education and family wealth. For the working-class American, who inhabits a more precarious world than the rich or the upper-middle class, family stability is a prerequisite for financial stability, and so working-class voters are less likely to benefit from greater sexual freedom and more likely to suffer from its side effects. From the 1970s onward, then, the crime wave and the Sexual Revolution pushed working-class life into a vicious cycle, in which family breakdown fed crime and disorder, and disorder fed family breakdown, and both trends led to economic difficulties for people without significant reserves of capital to fall back on. "The personal is political" was the famous radical chant of the era, and it was accurate enough—but it meant something very different for blue-collar Americans, and there were enough of them to tip the country substantially to the right.

The End of Equality

But it wasn't just crime and contraception turning working-class life sour in the seventies—it was the end of the postwar economic boom, which picked that decade to finally run out of steam. The turning point was 1973, the year that hourly wages, which had steadily risen for thirty years, began to stagnate or even fall. There was a recession, but the problem ran deeper than a temporary downturn: Globalization began to hurt American manufacturing as jobs slipped away overseas; rising immigration rates, following the 1964 reform, created a glut of low-wage labor; and skill-biased technological change meant that the market for employment increasingly privileged education over hard work. The great meritocratic experiment that had begun in the 1940s and '50s was coming into its own, but it wasn't working out exactly as expected: Instead of ushering in ever-increasing economic parity, it was breeding inequality and stratification.

In the nineteenth century, as we have seen, America's unprecedented economic equality rested on the widespread ownership of land; in the twentieth, on the universality of labor. In the Space Age, egalitarianism was supposed to be based on universal education. Policies like the G.I. Bill and the Pell Grant would make a college degree as common as a high-school diploma, with the same opportunities available to every American irrespective of his socioeconomic roots. At first, the transformation seemed to work: Across the fifties and sixties, college went from being the preserve of the leisure class to an increasingly important aspect of the American dream, while wages for high-school graduates remained high. It was the best of both worlds, but it didn't last.

Beginning in the mid-1970s, around the same time that working-class wages started stagnating and returns on a high-school diploma went into decline, higher education's steady spread began to slow. The share of American twentysomethings with a college degree leaped from 7 percent in 1940 to 27 percent in 1975—but then it began to level off and then to fall, dropping to 22 percent in 1995 before recovering to 27 percent again by 2004. (Similarly, the number of doctorates issued by U.S. colleges and universities leveled off completely in the 1970s; it began to climb again in the 1990s, but nearly all of that growth was explained by the presence of foreign students on temporary visas.)

This stratification by education was the dark side of meritocracy. A system that was supposed to make it easier for the deserving to rise and the undeserving to fall was hardening into the means by which an educated elite perpetuated itself, passing on social capital, great expectations, and SAT prep classes to its offspring, and creating a cycle of privilege nearly as powerful as the old WASP episcopacy it replaced. And the other trends of the era fed on one another to solidify the new social hierarchy. The crime wave and the drug culture threw up extra stumbling blocks to the poor and working class's ability to rise: Kids in Connecticut prep schools smoked pot and went on to college like their parents; kids in rural Indiana smoked meth and dropped out; kids in the South Bronx smoked crack and died in gang wars. The sexual revolution weakened working-class families at a time when, as the economist Arthur Kling put it recently, the economy was evolving "in ways that reinforce the financial differences between strong families and weak families." And in the new sexual landscape, marriage itself was increasingly segregated by class, as the educated married the educated and rarely looked down the social ladder for a mate, a phenomenon called "assortative mating" that ratified existing privilege and, as David Brooks has pointed out, turned the wedding pages of major newspapers into something resembling a list of law-firm mergers.

This hardening of the meritocratic arteries, combined with the globalization of labor, turned all the indicators of working-class life bad. Crime was rising, families were dissolving, and the economy wasn't generating the kind of wealth that could keep Americans moving upward even as their homes and neighborhoods dragged them down. Instead of a picket fence that was tallest in the middle, the American income distribution in the three decades after 1973 slowly shifted toward an inverted bell curve, with a mass upper-middle class (the beneficiaries of meritocracy and skill-biased technological change, and the people most likely to put their newfound personal freedom to good use) on one side of the divide, the working class on the other, and a shrinking middle in between.

In theory, these economic trends—the emerging "end of equality," as Mickey Kaus called it, memorably, in his 1991 book on the subject—could have benefited the Democrats, just as rising crime and familial disarray benefited the law-and-order, moralizing GOP that Goldwater had anticipated. Liberals might no longer be the advocates of New Deal maternalism, defending the sanctity of the family and the safety of the streets, but they were still the party of redistribution and economic justice, and here, at least, they seemed to have something to offer their longtime constituents in the working class—a helping hand in a time of financial need and a party that cared about using government power to advance the cause of equality, by tacking against the prevailing economic winds.

Sure enough, from the 1960s on, the very poor became steadily *more* likely to vote Democratic, as Democrats from Ted Kennedy down to Bill Clinton took up the new inequality as a rallying cry. But this wasn't enough to keep the working class in the liberal corner. Blue-collar voters were struggling for the first time since the Second World War, but they were hardly immiserated, as liberal rhetoric often seemed to suggest; non–college-educated voters might not be moving up the income ladder, but they were still better off than any working class in recorded history. These voters were receptive to economic populism (as the success of George Wallace in '68, and then Ross Perot a generation later, made clear), but they weren't particularly receptive to the kind of tax-and-transfer redistributionism that the Democrats of the 1970s and '80s were associated with, because it seemed primarily aimed at taking money out of their pockets and handing it out to the undeserving poor.

Blue-collar voters were the *working* class, after all, and the genius of the New Deal had been to use government power to help those who helped themselves—to offer a helping hand to people clambering up the ladder, rather than lavishing subsidies on the indigent. If you had a job, in the New Deal dispensation, you received Social Security benefits. If you saved for a home, you earned a home-mortgage deduction. If you worked hard and played by the rules, you received a pension, medical care, and a large enough salary that your wife could afford to stay home with the kids.

Lyndon Johnson's Great Society programs, by contrast, often eliminated the coercive and moralistic element from government spending, and as a result, working-class voters felt themselves to be subsidizing a growing, failing welfare system that cost them money and seemed to undermine their values into the bargain. As a young Republican strategist put it as early as 1969, the "Democratic Party fell victim to the ideological impetus of a liberalism which had carried it beyond programs taxing the few for the benefit of the many (the New Deal) to programs taxing the many on behalf of the few."

As a result, when their wages stagnated and the economy slowed down, they didn't demand more government spending— they demanded less, and the lower taxes that went with it. The tax revolts of the 1970s were first ignited by the kind of voters who had backed Goldwater in 1964—the "suburban warriors," as Lisa McGirr has called them, in prosperous areas like Orange County. But the antitax movement succeeded because working-class voters joined in. After thirty years of seeing government as their ally in the quest for prosperity and self-sufficiency, they looked at what the Democrats seemed to be selling—dependency, rather than independence; condescension, rather than solidarity—and said thanks but no thanks.

The Polarized Culture

They said no thanks, as well, to the culture and attitudes of liberalism's new elite—the children of meritocracy's first wave, who were college students in the sixties and seventies and constituted something new under the sun, the world's first mass upper class. "We are people of this generation, bred in at least modest comfort, housed now in universities, looking uncomfortably to the world we inherit," the Students for a Democratic Society put it in 1962, in their Port Huron Statement, and though the "modest" understated things a bit, a better summary of the New Class's genesis has rarely been offered. Loathed by conservatives, lionized by liberals, the young elites who began entering American life in the 1960s were neither so bad nor so heroic as their enemies and friends, respectively, would later claim. They were idealistic, certainly, and creative and sometimes even inspired; they were also narcissistic and reckless and self-destructive. But more than anything, they were distinguished by their rejection of the old common culture of the 1950s, the values and tastes that held sway irrespective of education or social class—Puritanism and patriotism, *Time* magazine and the Book-of-the-Month Club, opera broadcasts on the major networks, and Norman Rockwell illustrations on the cover of the weekly magazines.

In the short run, this rejection inspired a bohemian assault on middlebrow culture, which came in overlapping waves from the late 1950s onward, as the sneers of Clement Greenberg and Dwight Macdonald were succeeded by the Amerika-bashing of the antiwar movement, which gave way in turn to the rise of multiculturalism, PC, and chants of "Hey, hey, ho, ho, Western Civ has got to go." These provocations, particularly the antipatriotic ethos that emerged from the Vietnam debacle, contributed mightily to the cleavage between the working class and post-sixties liberalism, but more significant still was the cultural stratification that followed and that mirrored the larger stratification—by family stability, public safety, education, and wealth—taking place from the 1960s onward.

Some of this polarization was the inevitable result of technological change, which shattered the old monopoly that a few networks and magazines and studios enjoyed over midcentury American life. In the old dispensation, the highbrow and the lowbrow were forced to meet in the middle, because most cultural outlets were essentially middlebrow. In the post-1970s landscape, cable television and then the Internet meant that Americans were increasingly free to "cultivate their own cultural gardens," as the critic Terry Teachout phrases it, and the result was a country with more pornography and more Christian pop music; crummier mass-market magazines but a dizzying array of artsy Web sites; television shows far more sophisticated than anything 1965 had to offer and movies that are unimaginably crude by the old standards; fewer political columnists with the influence of a Walter Lippmann or a Scotty Reston but infinitely more political writers, and bloggers, and talking heads, all clamoring for attention.

But out of this chaos, a broader division emerged, splitting America into two cultures—one highbrow and one lowbrow; one elite and one largely working class; one the culture of the mass upper class, the winners in the meritocratic game (David Brooks's Bobos, Richard Florida's "creative class") and the other the common culture that the new elite had risen above or deliberately abandoned.

This cultural polarization was driven by ideology, in part. The radicalism of the sixties passed, but the meritocrats remained deeply suspicious of overt patriotism even as they mellowed into a respectable middle age; their deepest beliefs turned "spiritual" or secular rather than religious, and they dismissed most orthodox religion as an anachronism; they supported the sexual revolution without hesitation or regret and welcomed the gay rights movement when it emerged in the 1980s. All of these issues and more served to separate them from their erstwhile allies in the working class.

But it would also be driven by geography and lifestyle, and these would prove perhaps the more important factors. As America grew more stratified by educational attainment, it grew more segregated by education as well, with college graduates flocking to a relatively small set of cities, towns, and metropolitan areas, either on the two coasts or in the vicinity of major universities. In these overclass communities, the hard-edged anti-Americanism of the sixties gave way to a comfortable cosmopolitanism, a postnationalist mind-set that reflected the increasingly global landscape in which America's mass upper class moved and breathed. By 1990, this process was far enough advanced that Christopher Lasch could write, in his *Revolt of the Elites*:

> The upper middle class, the heart of the new professional and managerial elites, is defined, apart from its rapidly rising income, not so much by its ideology as by a way of life that distinguishes it, more and more unmistakably, from the rest of the population . . . The market in which the new elites operate is now international in scope. Their fortunes are tied to enterprises that operate across national boundaries . . . Their loyalties—if the term is not itself anachronistic in this context—are international rather than regional, national, or local.

This was a dyspeptic assessment, but not without some truth. This geographical and cultural polarization would be self-reinforcing. The more America's elites withdrew into their comfortable enclaves, the more coarsened and disrupted life became for the working-class voters who couldn't make their way into the charmed circle of university towns and financial centers, and who were stuck with soaring crime rates, rising illegitimacy and drug use, and all the other scourges that followed in the sixties' wake. The coarser and darker working-class life became, in turn, the more determined the overclass became to segregate themselves (and their children) from the rest of American society, which they increasingly regarded as at once "absurd and vaguely menacing," as Lasch put it, filled with "fanatical religiosity . . . a repressive sexuality that occasionally erupts into violence against women and gays, and in a patriotism that supports imperialist wars and a national ethic of aggressive masculinity."

This pattern would play itself out across every arena of American culture. As the educated class became dismissive of religious faith, the religious traditions they had abandoned turned increasingly anti-intellectual, with Tim LaHaye and Jerry Falwell succeeding Reinhold Niebuhr and Thomas Merton; this, in turn, made America's meritocrats more contemptuous still toward organized religion. As highly educated consumers abandoned *Newsweek* and the networks in favor of the more highbrow pleasures afforded by cable television and NPR and HBO, the mass-market magazines and national networks turned to bread and circuses—game shows and blockbuster movie covers, reality TV and self-help columns—to keep their audiences hooked, which only encouraged further defections by their highbrow readers and further cultural polarization. The more that elites kept patriotism at arm's length and treated national pride with a sophisticate's tolerance, the more the breach was filled by Sean Hannity–style jingoists. The more the mass upper class seemed to look down on the rubes in "Red America," the more the rubes returned the favor, embracing a self-conscious anti-intellectualism that ran from George Wallace down through to Ross Perot and reached its apotheosis, perhaps, in the era of George W. Bush.

As the examples of Wallace and Perot suggest, this cultural

polarization didn't necessarily have to benefit the GOP. In theory, at least, the Democrats have had as many chances as the Republicans to ride anti-elitism to a political majority by attacking those aspects of the elite consensus—free trade, deregulation, privatization—that dovetailed with the GOP's positions and often cost working-class voters their jobs. The emerging mass upper class included plenty of juicy Republican targets for blue-collar ire: Ken Lay was part of the new transnational elite; so was Michael Milken. As David Brooks pointed out, the political divide of 2006 pitted a "ranch-owning millionaire Republican like George Bush" against a "vineyard-owning millionaire Democrat like Nancy Pelosi," in a "clash of the rival elites, with the dollars from Brookline battling dollars from Dallas." In this landscape, populism could easily cut both ways.

But in practice, the overclass's public face—academics and actors, journalists and bureaucrats, scientists and filmmakers and social workers—was liberal and Democratic, and try as it might, liberalism couldn't escape its identification with the elitist side of an increasingly polarized culture. Crime and the courts and divorce and illegitimacy and abortion and failed welfare policies and high tax rates and all the other issues that dominated discussion from the late sixties onward pushed the New Deal majority to the brink, but it was this cultural polarization that sealed the old consensus's fate. For thirty-five years after the watershed of 1968, from the Vietnam War protests down to the battles over *The Passion of the Christ*, a wall of misunderstanding, fear, and hatred would divide working-class Americans from the nation's best and brightest, and no left-of-center politician would find a permanent way to scale it. There might be another Democratic majority waiting to be built, but from the late sixties onward, Roosevelt's coalition—of blacks and whites, the mandarins and the masses—was finished.

3

In Search of a New Majority

If the old majority was finished, what would replace it? As the New Deal coalition broke apart in the late 1960s, two young strategists—one conservative and one liberal—offered competing visions of the country's political future.

The more famous of the two belonged to Kevin Phillips, whose 1969 treatise *The Emerging Republican Majority* quickly became known as the "political Bible of the Nixon years." Phillips argued that the working class's rightward turn was the defining event of the era, promising a Republican majority that combined Goldwater voters with the millions of blue-collar Americans fleeing the Democratic Party over crime, values, and the Great Society. It would be a majority whose strength was concentrated in the South and West, in the suburbs and the growing cities of the Sun Belt, where non–college-educated Americans were moving as they moved up in the income ladder and their old urban neighborhoods decayed. And it would leave the Democrats stuck with a minority coalition of union employees, minorities, and what Phillips termed "silk stocking" voters—the upper-class voters who were turning leftward on race and lifestyle questions.

The Emerging Republican Majority is one of the best-known books in American political history, and one of the least understood. Phillips didn't argue for a "Southern strategy" built on antiblack backlash, as is often suggested; indeed, for most of the book's four hundred pages he didn't really argue for any strategy at all, confining himself to a meticulous description of political trends across all fifty states. He did take for granted the Deep South's move out of the Democratic column, but insofar as he made recommendations to the Republican Party, they were the opposite of the kind of race-baiting strategy that liberals have accused him of advocating. The GOP, he pointed out, didn't need "to bid much ideologically" to get the votes of die-hard segregationists, who had nowhere else to go; indeed, because the "Deep South must soon go to the national GOP," it was in the Republicans' interest to focus their efforts on winning working-class voters in the West, the Border South, and the suburban Northeast, and take the heart of Dixie for granted. As Gerald Alexander has pointed out, in a lengthy *Claremont Review of Books* attack on "The Myth of the Racist Republicans," Phillips thought that the party's inroads elsewhere "would bring the Deep South along in time, but emphatically on the national GOP's terms, not the segregationists'."

More broadly, Phillips argued that the new majority he had outlined, while technically "conservative," actually represented a more progressive impulse than the Great Society liberalism it was replacing. "Whatever limousine liberalism says," he pointed out, the South and West "is not reactionary country. On the contrary, it has been the seat of every popular, progressive upheaval in American politics—Jefferson, Jackson, Bryan, Roosevelt." Phillips hoped for a new majority in this tradition, which would "overthrow the obsolescent 'liberal' ideology and interests of today's Establishment" and pursue "policies able to resurrect the vitality and commitment of Middle America— from sharecroppers and truckers to the alienated lower middle classes." It was a vision of a Sam's Club majority, in a sense, fifteen years before Sam's Club even existed.

While Phillips was calling for a GOP majority built on working-class support, a little-remembered Democratic strategist was envisioning a future for his party that didn't involve the working class at all. In 1971, two years after *The Emerging Republican Majority* appeared, a Californian named Fred Dutton—Bobby Kennedy's campaign manager—authored a short book called *Changing Sources of Power: American Politics in the 1970s.* Like Phillips, he foresaw the crack-up of the aging New Deal coalition, but he argued that the Democrats would be better off without the old working-class groups—white ethnics, and particularly white ethnic Catholics—that had been bastions of Democratic support ever since Roosevelt. They were yesterday's news, stuck with yesterday's ideas. "The net effect of these groups in relation to the dynamic of social change has become vastly different from thirty or sixty years ago," Dutton argued. "Then they were a wellspring of cultural diversity and political change; now they constitute an important bastion of opposition. They have tended, in fact, to become a major redoubt of traditional Americanism and of the antinegro, anti-youth vote."

It was on the youth, above all, that Dutton placed his hopes for the next majority, particularly the upper-middle-class youth filling colleges and universities. As he put it in a confidential 1969 letter:

With the profound alienation now apparent in this country, on the left, middle, and right, the party should harness the widespread want for involvement and participation by rank-and-file people in the larger questions affecting their lives, including the full range of economic, social, bureaucratic, yes, and nuclear issues disturbing them. Fortunately, winning elections and giving expression to those insurgent impulses reinforce each other in the better educated, more affluent, and activist society. That is especially true among younger voters, black citizens, and college-educated suburbanites—three constituencies on which the Democratic Party must build as the lower-middle-class, blue-collar vote erodes. Some of that erosion is caused in a short-term sense by racial and generational tensions. But the traditional blue-collar base, while still very substantial politically, is disappearing over the long run by losing most of its children into a different political and social group with rising educational levels, affluence, and the greater cultural sophistication taking hold.

The Democrats would lose working-class parents, in this theory, by turning leftward on all the hot-button issues of the day, but they would win the children—who were better-educated than their parents, and therefore more liberal. And in winning them, they would win the future.

Phillips had charts and graphs and meticulous analysis; Dutton had power. From 1969 to 1972, he served on a Democratic commission chaired by Senator George McGovern of South Dakota, whose twenty-eight members were charged with reshaping how the Democrats went about picking their presidential nominees. In the words of Mark Stricherz, who examined Dutton's legacy in his provocative book *Why the Democrats Are Blue*, his goal "was nothing less than to end the New Deal coalition, the electoral alliance that had supported the party since 1932 around a broad working-class agenda. In its place, Dutton sought to build a 'loose peace constituency,' a collection of groups opposed to the Vietnam War and more generally the military-industrial complex."

To accomplish this end, the commission broke the power of the old party bosses—the machine politicians, typically representatives of the urban working class, who had engineered nominations in smoke-filled rooms for generations. As the role of these insiders was reduced, the power of primary voters was expanded, and so was the role of Dutton's favored constituencies: By 1972, the Democratic Party's nominating rules included quotas for youth delegates, along with blacks and women. The result, in the '72 election, was the first collision of the two visions that would shape American politics for a generation—a Republican Party trying to appeal to working-class voters and a Democratic Party trying to do without them. And the outcome of the race, of course, was a triumph for the GOP and a debacle for the Democrats.

McGovern himself was something of a misunderstood figure, and in a different context he might have been able to attract significant support from working-class Democrats. He was a prairie populist who attacked "bloated bureaucracies" and promised to "decentralize our system," while denouncing the sins of "the establishment wise men, the academicians of the center" in forgotten campaign speeches that partake more of George Wallace than Ted Kennedy. But in the context of the '72 race, McGovern was perceived—accurately enough—as the candidate of Dutton's left-wing vanguard, the confident liberal boomers who swarmed over the Democratic National Convention, producing a platform that reads like a parody of sixties liberalism.

This New Left potpourri would have doomed Dutton's Democrats anyway, but it was pitted against the political skill of Richard Nixon, who engineered (through fair means and foul) a landslide victory of epic proportions. He had won the presidency in 1968 because George Wallace stole working-class votes from the Democratic column; in 1972, he took those working-class votes for his party and himself. In both elections, he became the first beneficiary of the realignment that Phillips had described, and the architect of a working-class conservatism that would shape American politics for the next quarter century.

Nixon's Lost Opportunity

As Nixon took office, it was clear that economic trends were going to put the squeeze on a growing number of blue-collar workers, even as the era's collapsing social order carried many working-class families down with it. With this pervasive unease in mind, Kevin Phillips called upon Nixon to embrace the "type of expansive economics which would put the needs of Middle America ahead perhaps of the needs of the board room," and Nixon, to his credit, listened closely. He understood that in times of wrenching economic change, counseling a politics of retrenchment and fiscal discipline inevitably places conservatives on the defensive. Only by offering a positive program can conservatives seize the political high ground.

Faced with a country that was coming apart along racial and cultural lines, Nixon sought to reconcile the ideological conservatism (the enduring belief in self-reliance) and the operational liberalism (the strong support for social welfare programs) of the American public, and in the process to build a new majority. To devise such a program, and to detach white ethnics and labor families from the crumbling New Deal coalition, the Nixon White House first turned to the idiosyncratic liberal intellectual Daniel Patrick Moynihan. A policy visionary, Moynihan saw Nixon as an ideal vessel for sweeping reforms. As Benjamin Disraeli might have put it, Nixon would be the "Tory man" for Moynihan's own "Whig measures," the most daring of which was the Family Assistance Plan, or FAP.

FAP was, in a sense, the first and most ambitious attempt at welfare reform. The measure combined a guaranteed annual income—a notion that, ironically enough, would later be revived by McGovern—with strict work requirements. It aimed to replace the whole constellation of bureaucratically administered programs, from Aid to Families with Dependent Children to food stamps and Medicaid, with direct cash payments. (In this, it drew on Milton Friedman's concept of a negative income tax and anticipated Charles Murray's recent proposal to replace the whole welfare state with a check-writing office.) The working poor as well as the jobless would qualify for its benefits, and every recipient save mothers with preschool children would be required to either work or take job training.

On paper, FAP was ingenious, and it dovetailed with more than a few Nixonian themes. Though it would increase welfare expenditures, it would spread much of the largesse among the blue-collar workers Nixon hoped to win over to the Republican side. But FAP did more than reward potential GOP constituents: It promised to dramatically prune the welfare bureaucracy, whose members Nixon regarded, not without reason, as entrenched left-wingers who would stymie his efforts at every turn—and, worse yet, would never dream of voting Republican. By sending checks directly to families, FAP would cut out the liberal middlemen and curb the growth of the administrative state. It was to be the linchpin of what Nixon termed his "New Federalism"—a sustained attempt to devolve power away from unelected bureaucrats and empower states, localities, and individuals.

But it went nowhere. Despite the drawdown of American forces from Vietnam, which reduced the record military expenditures that endangered LBJ's Great Society initiatives, there was little budgetary room for maneuver. And Nixon's attempt to steer between Goldwater conservatism and Great Society liberalism, inevitably, took heavy fire from Right and Left alike. Bureaucrats and caseworkers, fearing for their jobs, denounced the proposal; the Left attacked FAP for its stinginess (it allocated $1,600 per year for a family of four); while conservatives were wary of directing any more largesse to the poor, and particularly to poor urban blacks. The plan withered on the vine, and Nixon abandoned it by the 1972 election.

The FAP wasn't his last opportunity for domestic-policy innovation. In 1970, Jerome Rosow, the exhaustively titled assistant secretary of labor for policy, evaluation, and research, released a report on the "anxious Americans," the third of American families living, in the words of the report, "above the poverty line but below what is required to meet moderate family budget needs." This was somewhat exaggerated: When Franklin Delano Roosevelt declared, "I see one-third ill-housed, ill-clad, ill-nourished," he could not have known that the children of that same third would be so comparatively prosperous, with homeownership increasingly common and hunger all but vanquished. Nevertheless, the families described in the Rosow Report had real concerns—the erosion of their earning power, the rising crime that plagued their urban and inner-suburb neighborhoods, and the mounting sense that aid for the poor came out of their paychecks. To meet these challenges, Rosow proposed a reform agenda even more comprehensive than Moynihan's, tailored to the concerns of *all* working-class families. As Robert Mason writes, in *Richard Nixon and the Quest for a New Majority*:

> [Rosow's] suggestions included the enlargement of access to education, the provision of funds to childcare facilities, reforms of tax policy, regulation of workplace conditions, and attention to the government's status as a "model employer." Rosow also advocated action to restore the status of blue-collar work. "These frustrated individuals, caught in a situation from which they see no escape, are likely to vent their feelings in actions harmful to both themselves and society," he wrote. "Beyond that, our system of values signals that something is very wrong when conscientious, able, and hardworking people cannot make it."

The Rosow plan was less than ideal in many respects, but as this quotation suggests, it made the crucial distinction between the deserving and the undeserving poor, between government programs that build self-reliance and those that breed dependency. This distinction animated Roosevelt's working-class majority, and it was lost somewhere in the quest for the Great Society. In his rhetoric, Nixon grasped its power, and had he been able to translate it into policy, it might have been the foundation for an enduring right-of-center majority.

But the opportunity slipped away. Key voices in the White House backed the Rosow Report, including Moynihan and Chief of Staff Robert Haldeman, but it went nowhere thanks to stiff conservative opposition and, more fatally, a growing sense of complacency, as political appeals based largely on opposition to the counterculture and the antiwar Left proved potent enough to maintain the administration's popularity. Plans to solve what Nixon called the "massive crisis" in American health care were scrapped. Always more interested in foreign than domestic affairs, the president became a custodian of the very Great Society that he had run against, enforcing the busing policies the working class hated and dramatically expanding the civil rights bureaucracy, implementing the first significant affirmative action programs, and ramping up spending for precisely the kind of ineffective antipoverty programs that FAP had been designed to replace. Worse, the only "expansive economics" that he implemented were the worst sorts of statist pump-priming, calculated to address the needs of working-class voters just long enough to get him reelected.

Rather than build a new partisan majority on policy substance, Nixon built a *personal* majority on deep-seated working-class resentments. This made him the object of liberal hatred, in spite of his relatively liberal record, and conservative distrust, in spite of his conservative rhetoric. And it cost the Republican Party a chance to consolidate the majority that Phillips outlined and establish itself as the heir to the Roosevelt coalition. The GOP eventually outflanked the Democrats on a variety of other issues—taxes and welfare and crime, moral values at home and Cold War idealism abroad. But the problem of working-class insecurity, which Nixon identified and failed to address, lingers to the present day, persistently undercutting the GOP's attempts to consolidate the majority that he won for it.

The Right Comes of Age

In the aftermath of Watergate, the old political order was briefly restored. The Democrats won back the working class, capturing huge majorities in the midterms of 1974, and then took the White House in 1976, winning the South on Jimmy Carter's Georgia charm. For a fleeting moment, it seemed like liberals could have both their old working-class majority *and* Fred Dutton's boomer liberalism, embodied by the swarm of young politicians who surged into Congress in '74—the so-called "neo-liberals," who included future party luminaries like Gary Hart, Paul Tsongas, and Christopher Dodd. Conservatives, meanwhile, found themselves coping first with the gray mediocrity of Gerald Ford and then the unexpected success of Jimmy Carter, and many of them—including conservative activists like William Rusher, *National Review*'s publisher, and direct-mail pioneer Richard Viguerie—despaired of the GOP and speculated about the possibility of a third party.

When this party failed to emerge in '76, and Carter took the White House, it seemed that conservatism had failed. In a 1977 *Commentary* essay on the New Right, Jeane Kirkpatrick argued that Carter's victory demonstrated that the "voters will repudiate candidates who offer a narrowly ideological rhetoric and a divisive appeal," and that the Right's quest for a conservative majority was therefore doomed. Conservatives could win elections only when they faced off against an opponent, like McGovern, who was perceived as the "spokesman for a counterculture." In other circumstances, they would be inevitably defeated by candidates like Carter, who could project an "ideological ambiguity" that would reconcile conservatives and liberals, convincing each that he was on their side.

This was an accurate description of Carter's '76 campaign, a two-faced affair in which he promised (among other tergiversations) that he was in favor of "preserving the ethnic purity" of white neighborhoods while campaigning in working-class precincts, and then assured liberals that he backed integration. In a moment of political realignment, though, such "ideological ambiguity" could win elections but not a sustainable majority. There were too many contradictions involved in maintaining the Democratic coalition—reconciling socially conservative Southerners and Northern feminists, McGovernite doves and Scoop Jackson hawks, civil-rights activists and working-class welfare skeptics, and so on. And they meant that '74 and '76 were blips, the former created by Nixon's disgrace, the latter by Nixon's shadow, Ford's weaknesses, and Carter's all-things-to-all-people presidential campaign, which couldn't be sustained beyond the campaign trail. The Democrats could win working-class votes but couldn't hold on to them.

They couldn't hold religious voters, in particular—the working-class Catholics who had voted for Nixon, and the evangelical Christians who were reentering politics in an organized fashion for the first time since the Progressive Era, in response to the apparent disintegration of the country's social fabric, which many of them blamed on rising godlessness. The evangelicals had embraced Carter as one of their own in 1976, but they were inevitably disappointed by what they received in return. Abortion, in particular, was an issue that even the smoothest Democratic politician couldn't finesse. For the upper-middle-class meritocrats who had embraced the Sexual Revolution, it was a civil right; for the social conservatives who had once formed the core of the party's strength, it was a deal-breaker.

But there were other difficulties as well: Carter's IRS director, urged on by the civil-rights lobby, proposed that every private school founded after 1953 be stripped of its tax-exempt status (because they were all presumed to discriminate against blacks), a move that would have sunk a host of private Christian academies—and never mind that white Christian support had been crucial to the civil-rights movement's success in the 1960s South. Or again, two years later the White House Conference on Family—intended as a forum to address concerns about the breakdown of the two-parent family—had to be renamed the White House Conference on *Families*, so as to mollify liberals who favored the post–Sexual Revolution ideal of family as a "group of people living together." In response, social conservatives boycotted the conference and looked forward to supporting a president who "will be aggressive about bringing back traditional moral values," as Tim LaHaye put it after a particularly fruitless confab with Carter.

The Democrats couldn't hold the larger working class, either, in spite of continuing wage stagnation, the decline of the manufacturing sector, and the larger malaise that gripped the American economy in the Carter era. In a different world, these economic troubles might have made the working class more receptive (like many elites at the time) to the Left's solutions to the crisis—more enamored of government spending and even a European-style safety net, for instance, and more hostile to a seemingly failing capitalist order. Working-class voters, though, looked at the problems of the Carter presidency and saw liberal failures—wasteful spending, incompetent economic micromanaging, and pointless overtaxation. They saw what Mickey Kaus saw, describing the Democrats on election night in 1980:

The best minds of the Democratic party ran the liberal enterprise into the ground. They had put liberalism on the side of welfare rather than work. They funded housing projects that were among the most hellish places on earth.

74

They defended absurd extensions of criminals' rights. They funneled billions to big-city mayors who gave the money to developers who built hideous, bankrupt downtown malls. They let the teachers' union run the education department and the construction unions run the labor department.

They saw failure in foreign policy as well. Working-class life depends on solidarity not just in families and churches and neighborhoods, but in the nation as a whole, with patriotism as the glue holding the country's civic life together. And working-class voters observed in Carter what they'd feared in McGovern—a weakness that put this solidarity at risk.

Worse, they saw the consequences of this weakness first-hand, in the degradation of the U.S. military. The military had already been a heavily working-class institution during the Vietnam War, but it was even more working class once it went all-volunteer in 1973: The rich were no longer drafted in, and it became an obvious place for young people without the benefits of a college degree to find employment and better themselves in the process. Thus it was primarily the sons and daughters of working-class voters who experienced the demoralized, underfunded military of the latter 1970s—a military rife with drug use and recruitment problems, a military that had some 130,000 soldiers go AWOL in one form or another during 1977, a figure higher than the worst years of the Vietnam War. In the forties and fifties, the military was politically as well as socioeconomically diverse, but that changed in the Carter era. For those soldiers who didn't drop out—for their husbands and wives, parents and siblings—there was a lesson to be learned from the misery of the post-Vietnam army, and it was a lesson that cautioned against voting Democratic.

Perhaps most tellingly of all, the Democrats couldn't even retain the support of Jeane Kirkpatrick herself, or the rest of the once-liberal intellectuals, most of them Jews and Catholics, who turned right along with the working class, becoming the "neoconservatives" who would provide the American Right with the kind of credibility it had conspicuously lacked in the Goldwater era. The Old Right's intellectuals had been brilliant but marginal; the neoconservatives were defiantly mainstream, committed to the idea of a welfare state and wary of capitalism's excesses (Irving Kristol famously offered only "two cheers" for the system) but also eager to defend the distinctively American mix of social conservatism and self-reliance against the left-wing spirit of their age. More important, they were eager to defend America itself, and they perceived the same weakness in the Democratic Party that working-class voters did—a weakness embodied by Jimmy Carter's immortal words that what America most had to fear was "our inordinate fear of Communism."

The Nixon era, and especially the McGovern campaign, had begun these liberals' rightward shift; four years of weakness and waxing Soviet power under Carter completed it. In her *Commentary* essay, which was published in 1977, Kirkpatrick still felt the need to draw a major distinction between right-wingers like Rusher, Pat Buchanan, and others, who wanted to roll back the New Deal, and "intellectuals affiliated with the Democratic Party" like "Daniel Bell, Seymour Martin Lipset, Midge Decter, Michael Novak," and others (herself included), who were opposed to the errors of the new liberalism but weren't willing to take the plunge into Republicanism. The ideological distinction was real enough; the neoconservatives were supporters of the fifties biggish-government consensus, not right-wingers in the style of Goldwater or William F. Buckley. But it would soon prove a distinction without a political difference: Decter and Novak were two years away from becoming ardent Reaganites, and Kirkpatrick was three years away from becoming Reagan's ambassador to the United Nations.

The result of all these Democratic losses was a conservative movement swollen by ex-liberals. There were evangelical Christians who decided that abortion and family breakdown were more pressing social justice issues than subsidizing inner-city housing projects and passing the ERA; factory workers who signed up for the tax revolts of the late 1970s alongside their better-off neighbors; middle-class families hit hard by inflation-induced bracket creep; and neoconservatives who found a new right-of-center mainstream in between the Old Right and the New Left. Thus the elections of '78, in which the Democrats took a beating and saw their congressional majorities dwindle—and thus, too, the Reagan Revolution of 1980, which *Time* magazine called "one of the most astonishing political and personal triumphs in the nation's history," but which shouldn't have been surprising at all to anyone paying attention to the voting public's concerns.

Reagan's landslide unified the South and his native West in a Republican bloc and vindicated Kevin Phillips's theory, while making Fred Dutton's dream of a majority built around "younger voters, black citizens, and college-educated suburban-ites" look like a pathetic fantasy. As Dutton himself put it, years later, "young people didn't vote until they were thirty-five years old. And black leaders talked a good game [about delivering the black vote], but they didn't walk a good game." As for the college-educated suburbanites, they *were* trending toward the Democrats overall, but their leftward movement slowed to a crawl during the disastrous Carter years, as pocketbook concerns trumped their sympathies with liberals on sex and civil rights. Dutton's thesis had assumed an ever-growing population with college degrees, but by the late seventies, the share of young Americans getting a four-year diploma had leveled off and began to fall. Meritocracy was forging a socially liberal upper-middle class, sure enough, but the stratification it created kept this elite from constituting a majority, or anything close.

So while Carter's "inclusive" spirit, in Kirkpatrick's phrase, might have won him the White House, it was an expansive conservatism, suddenly occupying the American center, that had the last laugh four years later. Still, Kirkpatrick's essay got one thing right. The New Right, she had argued, "will fail in its current version because of its hostility to another deeply rooted aspect of contemporary politics—the welfare state, whose benefits no majority in any democratic country has yet foresworn." It didn't fail, but neither did Americans forswear the welfare state by voting for Reagan; indeed, his success was inversely proportional to how fiercely he preached the old-time Goldwater antigovernment religion.

It's true that the public's disgust with liberalism, and Carter's incompetence in particular, was strong enough that Reagan could win the White House while expressing a hostility to federal programs that would have been unthinkable a decade before. But while small-government conservatives rightly remember him as one of their own, he was at great pains to downplay his affinities for Goldwaterism during the latter stages of the '80 campaign. He would attack government waste and oppressive bureaucracy, but never the pillars of the welfare state. He would champion tax cuts, but do so while embracing supply-side theory, which held that slashing taxes would actually *increase* government revenues. Conservatives thought that cutting taxes might starve the beast; Reagan promised voters that cutting taxes would provide more than enough federal money to go around.

In unguarded moments, the Gipper might compare the New Deal to fascism, but when he accepted the GOP's nomination for president his speech quoted Franklin Delano Roosevelt and pledged to protect the "strength of the safety net beneath those in society who need help" and the "integrity of all aspects of Social Security." When he was sworn in as president, he prefaced his famous announcement that "government is the problem" with the qualifier "in the present crisis," a caveat that put him precisely in tune with working-class sentiment. And he followed it up with a statement that partook more of neoconservatism than it did of the Right's old abolish-the-TVA spirit: "Now, so there will be no misunderstanding, it's not my intention to do away with government. It is rather to make it work—work with us, not over us; to stand by our side, not ride on our back."

This was what working-class voters wanted to hear, and Nixon's Silent Majority was reborn as the Reagan Democrats. Both the college-educated and the very poor voted in roughly the same patterns in 1976 and 1980; what changed was the vote of those in between, the well-off working class. Blue-collar Americans in general broke three-to-two for Reagan; high-school graduates gave Reagan an eight-point edge after having gone for Carter by the same margin four years before. Even union families, the most reliably Democratic voters in the working-class population, voted for Carter by only six points, down from twenty-seven in '76. And it was a more impressive triumph even than Nixon's 1972 landslide, because Reagan's coattails carried the Senate for the GOP as well, breaking forty years of Democratic control.

"Our old enemy liberalism has died." So spoke Rusher, after the Reagan landslide. But it wasn't the Goldwater Right that had killed it off. It was the conservatism of Jews like Irving Kristol, Catholics like Michael Novak, and evangelicals like Jerry Falwell, none of whom would have voted Republican twenty years before. It was a conservatism that promised to fix the welfare state, rather than abolish it; to reform the Great Society, but leave the New Deal more or less intact. It was the conservatism of a working class that had swung to the GOP, not because they had been persuaded of the merits of the antigovernment Right's prescriptions, but because the Republicans seemed to better embody the consensus of the 1950s. The party's new constituents wanted the same thing from Reagan they had wanted from Nixon, and would want again from Newt Gingrich and George W. Bush: the government that the New Deal liberals had built, but run by conservatives.

The Reagan Years

In many ways, Reagan governed as he had campaigned—as a neoconservative, and the custodian of the working-class conservatism that Richard Nixon had captured. Conservatives flooded into the administration, but they were more likely to be "neos" than "paleos": In a representative incident, Reagan tapped a brilliant Old Right historian named Mel Bradford to head the National Endowment for the Humanities, only to withdraw the nomination over Bradford's Confederate sympathies and appoint Bill Bennett instead. Reagan called *National Review* his favorite magazine, but it was the neoconservative *Commentary* that probably had more influence on his policies, foreign and domestic alike.

In national security, there wasn't much room between the Old Right and the newer conservatives: Both cheered Reagan's defense buildup, his restoration of military morale, and his hard line against the Soviets; and both were disappointed when he (wisely) decided to trust Mikhail Gorbachev's glasnost in his second term. Still, Reagan's vision owed more to Truman and John F. Kennedy than to the more extreme conservatism of the fifties and sixties, with its confidence in "rollback" and its loose talk about nuclear war (which Reagan was famously horrified by).

On the domestic front, Reagan disappointed the small-government Right far more than he did either the neoconservatives or the GOP's newfound Reagan Democrat constituents. When Scoop Jackson was offered a place in the Reagan administration, he declined, saying "I still believe in the New Deal." Reagan probably didn't, but he governed as though he did. His sweeping tax cuts took a page from Goldwater's 1964 campaign, but the rest of his agenda deliberately avoided the kind of cuts in social spending that many right-wingers hoped that he would pursue. (Within a year of Reagan's inauguration, Richard Viguerie and others were already denouncing him as a crypto-liberal.) He continued the deregulation that had begun under Carter, and slowed the growth of social welfare spending—but not by that much, and certainly not to the extent that fiscal hawks would have liked. Entitlement spending wasn't touched at all, and the number of workers on the federal payroll inched upward; an abortive attempt to cut spending on Social Security helped produce GOP losses in the 1982 midterms and was never tried again. As Lou Cannon, the president's best biographer, has noted: "For all the fervor they created, the first-term Reagan budgets were mild manifestos devoid of revolutionary purpose."

Meanwhile, what spending cuts there were couldn't cover the cost of the Reagan defense buildup, resulting in the large-scale deficits that would become a recurring feature of Republican administrations. These deficits were not nearly so damaging to the country's fiscal health as many liberals claimed, suddenly discovering the virtues of fiscal conservatism, and there's no question that the tax cuts Reagan enacted changed the economy for the better, breaking the stagnant statism of the Ford and Carter years and producing the economic boom of the mid-1980s. But the tax cuts also proved the more expansive supply-siders wrong: Lower tax rates, even in an overtaxed country, couldn't pay for themselves. This contradiction forced Reagan to roll back some of his initial cuts—he raised taxes four times between 1982 and 1984, albeit never back to 1970s levels—and then to accept, in the sweeping Tax Reform of 1986, increases in corporate taxes that many right-wingers considered anathema.

Most voters didn't feel that way, of course, particularly the

Reagan Democrats; they were happy to accept a tax reform that lowered their taxes by closing corporate loopholes, and pleased when Reagan backed a program called the Earned Income Tax Credit, which effectively provided a wage subsidy for the working poor. (The EITC was a classic maternalist program, using government funds to encourage work and increase self-reliance; naturally, it was also a resounding success where most of the no-strings-attached Great Society programs had been failures.) Overall, the working class benefited from Reaganomics and the boom that it created, but not as much as might have been hoped. Unemployment fell, and the surging economy produced cheaper goods (the first Sam's Club opened in 1982) and higher standards of living for blue- and white-collar workers alike. But at the same time, the stagnating wages of the 1970s persisted.

Worse, the other social indicators were still pointing south: Crime dropped somewhat in the first half of the decade, thanks in part to tougher sentencing policies, but then the crack epidemic hit and lawlessness rose anew. The Moral Majority might have a direct line to the White House and porn might be high on the attorney general's agenda, but even a conservative White House could do little about divorce rates, rising illegitimacy, abortion, and STDs. The Right's thinkers were busy: The 1980s were an intellectual golden age for the neoconservatives, a time when a generation of social scientists (Charles Murray, James Q. Wilson, Thomas Sowell, and many others) made their names by proposing reforms to the welfare state. But it would be years before their proposals were enacted.

None of this kept Reagan from winning an even more sweeping mandate in 1984, against the disastrous candidacy of Walter Mondale. But the Democrats were feeling their way back from exile, as the neoliberals who had swept into office in the 1970s came of age and tempered the radicalism of the McGovern moment with the lessons of the seventies and early eighties. Out of these debacles came Democrats determined to accept the

necessity of lower taxes and freer markets and promise competence and innovation rather than the socialist dreams of Teddy
Kennedy. At their best, these neoliberals were centrists with an
edge, willing to contemplate radical ideas—from means-testing
Social Security to expanding patronage in government hiring—
in the name of moderation and post-partisanship. Through
magazines like the *Washington Monthly,* they pushed a liberalism that would spend more money than Carter or McGovern on
the military (though not so much as Reagan); that would hold
the welfare and education bureaucracies accountable (though
without necessarily cutting spending); that would regard organized labor's demands for higher wages with suspicion (but
without necessarily taking management's side); and that would
stop coddling criminals and accept the necessity of tougher
prison sentences (though not necessarily the death penalty).

Meanwhile, recognizing that what plagued the working class
wasn't poverty but a lack of security, opportunity, and cultural
confidence, their brightest minds tried to turn the Democratic
Party's emphasis from redistribution (what Mickey Kaus called
"money liberalism") toward a "civic liberalism" that would promote a more *socially* egalitarian society—a country in which
both rich and poor would have equal access to education and
health care, and a country where national-service programs (or
a revived military draft) and other bridge-builders would narrow the cultural chasm.

With this emphasis on innovation in the background, and
accusations that Reagan was presiding over a "Swiss cheese
economy" in the foreground, the Democrats recovered large
congressional majorities in 1986. This victory was supposed
to provide a stepping-stone to the White House in 1988, but
Michael Dukakis was a weak vessel (not for nothing had many
neoliberals preferred first Gary Hart and then Al Gore). Dukakis was the perfect candidate for the mass upper class—fiscally
conservative but culturally liberal, both opposed to the death

penalty and a card-carrying member of the ACLU, with anti-interventionist, post-patriotic foreign policy sympathies. As a result, he picked up votes in the college-educated demographic, just as Fred Dutton had prophesied fifteen years before—winning in places like Silicon Valley and San Mateo County in California and suburban New Jersey and Virginia in the East, where Reagan had trounced his Democratic opponents. And he used this uptick in upper-middle-class support to improve on Mondale and Carter's showings in what was increasingly the country's battleground area, capturing Minnesota, Wisconsin, and Iowa, and coming close in a number of other Midwestern states.

But it wasn't nearly enough. George H. W. Bush, patrician, tongue-tied, and without a populist bone in his body, couldn't quite match the kind of supermajorities of white working-class voters that Reagan had managed, but he still won 60 percent of what we can now begin to call the Sam's Club demographic, which was more than enough to keep the White House in Republican hands. Eight years of GOP dominance hadn't brought the decades-long crime wave to a halt, but Dukakis reminded working-class voters of everything the Democrats had done wrong on crime in the sixties and seventies—eschewing the death penalty, coddling convicts like Willie Horton, obsessing over civil liberties. The Cold War seemed to be winding down, but nobody was sure of it, and Dukakis was both a foreign-policy neophyte and a dove, and working-class voters knew it. Above all, they knew he wasn't one of them: George H. W. Bush was faking his populism, up to a point, but in the cultural divide between the country's working-class majority and its leadership class, Dukakis was emphatically, viscerally on the other side.

So Bush was swept into the presidency with a landslide nearly as large as Reagan's first, seemingly confirming conservatism's hold on power and setting it up for its ultimate vindication in foreign policy, which came with the collapse of the Berlin Wall in 1989 and then Soviet Communism itself two years later. "We win, they lose," Reagan had said when asked about his vision of the Cold War; a decade later, two conservative administrations presided over the fulfillment of this boast.

This victory, though, undermined his party's grasp on political power. As we have seen, Reagan had won over the American public to tax-cutting but not to the small-government agenda of his party's activists—and by winning the Cold War, he and his successor at once vindicated the Right and took one of the GOP's best issues off the table. In 1988, a quarter of Americans called foreign policy the most important issue facing the country; by 1992, that percentage was plunging toward zero. The shift ensured that the debates of the 1990s would focus on domestic policy, where the Democrats had lost working-class voters but the Republicans hadn't yet found a way to permanently win them. The Reagan years demonstrated that tax cuts alone weren't enough to solve the working class's difficulties, and the GOP still lacked "policies able to resurrect the vitality and commitment of Middle America," in Phillips's *Emerging Republican Majority* phrase. Meanwhile, after the Dukakis debacle, the neoliberal message was being honed to a sharper point, even as the 1980s boom began to run out of steam. Barely a decade after the Reagan Revolution, and with the 1992 election just around the corner, American politics would be up for grabs again.

4

The Conservative Nineties

The end of the Reagan era ushered in a period of American anxiety. With the Cold War won, Communism's defeat was quickly recast as a Pyrrhic victory, whose aftermath would consign victor and vanquished alike to the ash heap of history. America's star was in decline, historians and economists confidently declared, and the future would belong to the rising commercial powerhouses of Japan and Germany. Globalization was vacuuming American jobs south to Mexico or across the Pacific; multiculturalism and racial strife were tearing us apart at home. There were riots in Los Angeles, the worst since the 1970s. There were demagogues: Pat Buchanan and Jerry Brown in the 1992 primaries, and then Ross Perot in the general election. There was a recession.

Doomsayers seized the moment. Al Gore wrote *Earth in the Balance,* predicting ecological collapse and comparing pollution to National Socialism. Paul Ehrlich published *The Population Explosion,* a sequel to his 1970s jeremiad *The Population Bomb,* and recycled the earlier book's predictions of imminent apocalypse—pushed back a bit, naturally, to account for civilization's persistence in the interim. A host of commentators argued that the burgeoning federal deficit would swamp our economy by 2000, or 2020 at the latest. A war in the Middle East, under the aegis of the United Nations, offered ammunition to millenarians and Rapture-obsessives everywhere.

The defining novel of the era was Michael Crichton's *Rising Sun*, a yellow-peril thriller in which a lazy, spendthrift America has fallen under the thumb of crafty, "business-is-war" Japanese. The defining work of history was Paul Kennedy's *The Rise and Fall of the Great Powers*, which announced the end of American preeminence and suggested that the main task for American statesmen in the coming decades was to find a way to "manage" the erosion of their nation's influence. The defining movie, perhaps, was *Falling Down,* in which Michael Douglas's everyman character is laid off by a defense contractor and becomes an accidental vigilante, wandering through Los Angeles and taking on greedy Korean grocers, crazy gangbangers, panhandlers, country-clubbers, and neo-Nazis—the melting pot recast as a multicultural nightmare.

On the Right, in particular, the twilight glow of Reagan's last years gave way to a gloomy dusk. As foreign policy victories receded and conservatives turned their gaze to the domestic front, the movement's accomplishments suddenly seemed negligible. In *Dead Right,* his 1994 assessment of where conservatism stood, David Frum noted that "however heady the 1980s may have been to everyone else, they were for conservatives a testing and disillusioning time." The Democrats had been temporarily defeated, but their works were still untouched: The federal government was still the bureaucratic hydra of FDR and LBJ and Nixon, and even Carter-era cabinet departments (Education, Energy) had been left untouched by the Reagan reformers. Taxes had been slashed and the economy had boomed, but spending cuts hadn't followed, and so the deficit was spiraling upward.

Nor had conservatives succeeded in mending the country's

social fabric (a difficult task for politicians, to be sure). After a decade of GOP rule, crime was still rising and cities were still crumbling; the major metropolises were assumed to be ungovernable, and a new wave of young "super-predators" was expected to hit the streets within the decade. The Rodney King case, and then the O. J. Simpson verdict, suggested that America was more racially polarized than ever. The economic growth of the Reagan years hadn't trickled down to the inner city, the welfare system languished unreformed, and efforts to repeal affirmative action had come to naught. Immigrants weren't assimilating because nobody was teaching them English—and yet they kept coming, because nobody seemed to be guarding the border.

From every front in the culture war, the dispatches offered fodder for pessimists and prophets of decline. Teen pregnancy and illegitimacy were still rising, as were sexually transmitted diseases (with AIDS expanding into the heterosexual population); the marriage rate tumbled and the divorce rate climbed. The abortion rate was unchanged since the early 1980s, and in 1992 the Supreme Court—packed with Republican appointees—declined to overturn *Roe v. Wade*, dealing a seemingly mortal blow to the pro-life cause. Pornography was everywhere; homosexuality was going mainstream; the Spur Posse were sleeping their way through Southern California. In the universities, it was the high tide of theory, of postmodernism, of political correctness and speech codes and canon-bashing. In the public schools, test scores fell while Sacagawea and Harriet Tubman crowded out the Founding Fathers.

In this slough of despond, Irving Kristol spoke for many on the Right when he wrote:

There is no "after the Cold War" for me. So far from having ended, my cold war has increased in intensity, as sector after sector of American life has been ruthlessly corrupted

by the liberal ethos. It is an ethos that aims simultane-
ously at political and social collectivism on the one hand,
and moral anarchy on the other. It cannot win, but it can
make us all losers. We have, I do believe, reached a critical
turning point in the history of the American democracy.
Now that the other "Cold War" is over, the real cold war
has begun.

So too Pat Buchanan, in his "cultural war" speech at the
1992 GOP convention, which summoned up the specter of the
Rodney King riots:

The mob was heading in, to ransack and loot the apartments
of the terrified old men and women. When the troopers arrived, M-16s at the ready, the mob threatened and cursed,
but the mob retreated. It had met the one thing that could
stop it: force, rooted in justice, backed by courage.

Greater love than this hath no man than that he lay down
his life for his friend. Here were 19-year-old boys ready
to lay down their lives to stop a mob from molesting old
people they did not even know. And as they took back the
streets of LA, block by block, so we must take back our cities, and take back our culture, and take back our country.

Yet even as conservatives girded themselves for battle, their
moment seemed to have passed. Working-class voters didn't
want a culture war or a street fight; battered by globalization,
by recession and layoffs, by self-doubt and portents of decline,
they wanted jobs, and they wanted empathy. For twenty years,
the Right had insisted that the problems of family breakdown,
rising crime, and cultural decay were essentially moral problems, not economic ones, and that the crisis of the underclass
and the struggles of the working class couldn't be ameliorated

by ever-increasing government largesse. But the country had given conservatives twelve years in power, and the Right's approach to the crisis seemed to have failed. None of this made Americans nostalgic for the chaos of the seventies or the hubris of the Great Society, but it did provide an opening for the Democratic Party, and particularly for its neoliberal adherents.

The Neoliberal Moment

After Gary Hart's candidacy evaporated and Michael Dukakis went down to defeat, a new generation of neoliberals took center stage. They called themselves "New Democrats," and they were more likely to be from the South and West than their predecessors—which meant that their candidates were less technocratic, more populist, and more in tune with the concerns of cultural conservatives than the previous generation had been. Still, their differences with the first wave of neoliberals were largely cosmetic. They, too, distanced themselves from the radicalism of the McGovern moment: They were hawkish where the Democrats of '72 had been dovish and even pacifistic; self-consciously tough on crime where the McGovern generation had been obsessed with police brutality and criminals' rights; willing to contemplate "ending welfare as we know it" where the '72ers had wanted to set the United States on the road to socialism. And they, too, accepted the Reagan consensus on taxes and government spending; when they called for tax hikes they were always aimed only at the rich who "haven't paid their fair share," as Clinton would put it, with accompanying cuts for the middle and working classes.

At the same time, they still *were* the McGovernites, older and grayer and more realistic in their political aspirations. They were just the younger wave: Gary Hart had been McGovern's campaign manager, whereas Bill and Hillary Clinton rose from further down the rungs of the South Dakota senator's campaign. The Clinton administration was rife with campus Left-ies turned white-collar success stories, who had traded in the long hair and loose-fitting clothes for the corner office and the six-figure salary. Their attempt to move the party right, in this sense, wasn't just an effort to reconcile the Democrats to a new political climate—it was a reflection of their own gradual move from radicalism to the half-conservative, half-libertine ideology of bourgeois bohemianism.

Jesse Jackson derided the New Democrats as "Democrats for the leisure class," which wasn't quite fair—they had worked hard, God knows, to rise through the meritocracy and then stay at the top. But his gibe got at a central truth of the neoliberal moment, and the Clinton administration that they created—namely, that this was very much an ideology crafted by the upper-middle class, reflecting their concerns and their preju-dices in its mix of tough-on-crime posturing (they had kids now, after all!), liberal internationalism (they were a globalized elite, weren't they?), fiscal conservatism (no class warfare in the sub-urbs, thank you very much), and social liberalism (because the Sexual Revolution needed to be preserved).

The hope, though, was that neoliberalism was also something more than this—that it would prove at once sufficiently conser-vative on crime and welfare to "inoculate" liberalism against conservative attacks and lure working-class voters back to the Democratic fold, while also winning some country-club Repub-licans with its mix of fiscal sobriety and cultural liberalism, and *also* holding the rest of the Democratic coalition (blacks, union members, feminists, and so forth) together because they had nowhere else to go. This was a tough balance to strike. But if successful, such a balancing act promised the fulfillment, in some sense, of Fred Dutton's dream—a majority party built around the rising generation of the 1970s, who were now all grown up and ready to govern.

They were given the chance in 1992, but not because the

balancing act worked. Clinton's neoliberalism didn't win back the working class; rather, the Republicans lost it, to a big-eared Texan with a taste for pie charts and folksy aphorisms. Clinton took 39 percent of the white working-class vote, which was more than Bush's 38 percent but less, remarkably, than Dukakis had won four years before. The rest went to Ross Perot, who was willing to go where Republicans feared to tread and address the economic anxieties of working-class voters as well as their cultural concerns. His success was astonishing by third-party standards—at his peak, Perot was polling in the thirties—and demonstrated the extent to which Reaganism had failed to cement the working-class's loyalty to the GOP, and the extent to which their stagnating wages and increasing insecurity made them vulnerable to the siren song of economic nationalism. It demonstrated the limits of neoliberalism as well, which for all of Clinton's maneuverings couldn't regain the advantage that Democrats had once enjoyed among the working class.

Still, even if their triumph in the presidential balloting was less than complete, the Democrats swept the congressional voting, with working-class voters abandoning the GOP in numbers not seen since 1976. For Republicans, the Reagan era ended in ignominious defeat: After the 1992 election, the Democratic Party controlled every branch of government for the first time since the Carter era, and its majority seemed nearly unassailable—254 to 178 in the House of Representatives, 58 to 42 in the Senate. The conservative moment seemed to have passed, and Clinton and his coterie turned to the task of governing as though it were their birthright, and there had been no Reagan interregnum.

The Triumph of the Right

But by the end of the decade, everything had changed. Clinton had been contained if not defeated; the Republican Party held both houses of Congress for the first time since the era of Dwight Eisenhower; a right-of-center consensus held sway on everything from welfare and balanced budgets to free trade and out-of-wedlock births. When the decade began, globalization was a bogeyman and free trade a poison pill; America's major cities were considered ungovernable; and a Democratic president was setting out to nationalize health care. By 2000, venture capitalists were heroes and globalization a welcome guest; New York was the shining, tourist-friendly capital of the globalized world; and that same liberal president had signed welfare reform, discussed experimenting with private Social Security accounts, and admitted publicly that the "era of big government is over." It was not an era that left conservatives satisfied—Clinton's persistence saw to that. But it was a conservative decade nonetheless, in which the gains of the previous twenty years consolidated and the movement's political successes and intellectual insights translated into dramatic social change.

Ironically, it was Clinton himself—hailed, briefly, as the Saint George to Reagan's dragon—who did as much as any politician to make the 1990s a conservative era. His first-term incompetence, in particular, accomplished what Reagan's genius couldn't bring about—the end of Democratic dominance in the Congress. The media, at first cool to Clinton's candidacy, eventually came around and treated his victory over Bush as a generational triumph, the baby boomers' coming-of-age after the long dark night of Reaganism, and Clinton governed, at first, as though he believed his own press. In the process, he reminded working-class voters why they had deserted the Democratic Party in the first place—by proposing vast new entitlement programs (or having his wife propose them for him, which was itself an example, to many people, of feminist overreach), promoting lifestyle-liberal pet causes like gays in the military, and generally aping the lack of discipline and overattention to detail that

had undone Jimmy Carter, with a dash of baby-boomer entitlement thrown in. He didn't throw over neoliberalism entirely,
but he hewed to it on issues—NAFTA, in particular—that were
calculated to alienate precisely those Perot voters he needed to
strengthen his majority.

The press, liberal but fickle, turned on him soon enough, and
the country followed, with the working class leading the way. In
the 1994 election, practically all the non–college-educated voters who had pulled the lever for Perot delivered their votes to
Newt Gingrich's GOP, whose Contract with America brilliantly
co-opted the Perot message and brought the Republicans, at
last, to the congressional majority that they had so ardently
desired. In later years, nostalgic conservatives would convince
themselves that the Contract with America was a document
of Goldwater-style small-government purity; in reality, it was
closer to neoconservatism, offering a laundry list of ideas to
make government work better, not pare it to the bone. There
were calls for welfare reform and attempts to curb illegitimacy,
for better-funded law enforcement and stricter sentencing, for
tax cuts targeted to working families and small businesses, for
term limits and a balanced-budget amendment, for giving parents more control over their children's education, and so on.
The Gingrich revolutionaries weren't neocons, exactly, but
their ideas were neoconservatism in action: a pragmatic rather
than ideological conservatism, targeted explicitly to voters who
wanted to keep the welfare state in place but didn't want the
Democrats to run it.

But Clinton didn't just deliver the GOP its long-dreamed-of
congressional majority; he also enabled conservatives to consolidate their gains by triangulating his way rightward to meet
them. Rather than casting himself as the leader of the liberal
opposition, he governed from the center-right, and confirmed,
by his very success, that this was a conservative era indeed.

And his triangulation opened space for pragmatic conservatism to flourish on the state and local level—an applied neoconservatism whose right-of-center reforms reshaped the welfare state for the better, and particularly the betterment of the working class.

Neoconservatism in Action

The most successful of these applied neoconservatives was also, in many respects, the most unlikely. As an intellectual movement, neoconservatism was urbane and self-consciously intellectual. Tommy Thompson, governor of Wisconsin from 1987 to 2001, was neither of these things. Hailing from Elroy, Wisconsin, a city of 1,500, he was known as "Dr. No" during his time as leader of the Assembly's Republican minority, where he aggressively championed taxpayers and small business, making him a rare Sun Belt–style partisan in the sleepily progressive Upper Midwest. Despite Ronald Reagan's political triumphs at the national level, Wisconsin was hardly the most hospitable terrain for Reaganism—the state was, after all, at the heart of the Rust Belt, and it had been bleeding manufacturing jobs almost as fast as it was bleeding families to the South and West. When Thompson won the governor's mansion, there was good reason to think his tenure would be brief.

Instead, he lasted fourteen years in office and transformed Wisconsin by pushing conservative ends through ideologically ambidextrous means. You might say Thompson made a virtue out of necessity. Ever since the La Follettes made Wisconsin a beacon of social policy innovation, the state had been enamored of rule by experts (usually the soft socialists of the University of Wisconsin), a technocratic settlement celebrated as the "Wisconsin Idea." Thanks in part to this legacy, the state offered generous welfare benefits that drew in poor mothers from Chicago and beyond. By 1987, Wisconsin offered the fifth most generous AFDC grant in the country, at a time when the state was battered by job losses.

Eventually, the technocrats began to adjust to the failures of the Great Society: Throughout the 1980s, scholars from the University of Wisconsin experimented with measures designed to encourage low-wage work, including a generous state-earned income tax credit. A Wisconsin professor of social work, Irwin Garfinkel, devised a child-support enforcement program that garnished the wages of deadbeat dads. But the caseload continued to increase, cresting at 300,000 in 1986, not coincidentally the year that Thompson was elected governor.

There was a pervasive sense, among liberals as well as conservatives, that the welfare system had failed. But the Wisconsin Idea remained powerful, and so Thompson framed welfare reform not as a measure aimed at punishing welfare families for being poor, but rather as a way to reconcile public assistance with Wisconsin values. He spoke the language of a tough-minded egalitarianism: If work was good enough for families struggling to stay in the middle class, it was good enough for welfare mothers. And he wasn't afraid to spend more money to achieve his ends: Indeed, Thompson managed the unexpected feat of sharply increasing public spending on the poor while also increasing working-class support for poverty-fighting programs—because for the first time in a generation, they seemed to be working.

This was not the playbook of Barry Goldwater. Shortly after Thompson came into office, for instance, he instituted a program called Learnfare, which cut AFDC grants to the families of teenagers who failed to stay in school. But rather than economize on welfare benefits, the program demanded considerable new spending to maintain accurate records and to take into account extenuating circumstances. So while Learnfare led to a $3 million reduction in welfare grants, it cost $14 million to make the program work.

But work it did, as welfare rolls began a steady decline. Truly sweeping change, though, came to Wisconsin only when the Clinton administration granted key federal waivers that enabled more significant experimentation. In 1993, Thompson took the radical and much-derided step of imposing a time limit on aid in two counties, a measure that proved successful enough to go statewide. The next year, the state started experimenting with early intervention programs to help families in need before they went on welfare, an approach that evolved into a statewide requirement that all applicants for assistance engage in an exhaustive job search before being declared eligible—a requirement that was strictly enforced.

By 1997, the caseload had declined by 65 percent over Thompson's time in office. But instead of resting on his laurels, Thompson then launched an even more ambitious program, Wisconsin Works, better known as W-2. The program flatly declared that assistance would no longer be granted on the basis of need alone. It would be earned, through participation in subsidized private sector jobs or public jobs for those without work experience. Treatment programs were offered to those addicted to drugs, but only *in addition to* full-time work. All aid recipients were given a flat grant, regardless of the number of children. At the same time, families were offered child care and generous health-care benefits that remained in place long after they left the welfare rolls. Other programs provided targeted interventions, including psychological counseling and job training for those who needed it. And the booming Wisconsin economy absorbed former recipients at a rapid rate: In its first year, the program cut welfare rolls by 70 percent.

All this success cost money. State spending during Thompson's tenure doubled, and the number of public employees increased. But the programs did what they set out to do: Instead of just pushing families off the welfare rolls, for instance, W-2 remained engaged in the lives of former recipients in an effort to help them move steadily up the earnings ladder. It was the old maternalist idea of using government policy not "to do things for a family," but rather "to create a family that can do things for itself." And it was an achievement that served as a model for state-level reforms across the country.

It was figures like Thompson—reformist Republican governors like John Engler in Michigan, reformist Republican mayors like Rudy Giuliani in New York—who achieved the greatest conservative victories in the 1990s; it wasn't, tellingly, the more strident government-cutters in the House of Representatives, who led their party to defeat in its battles with Bill Clinton. As a result of the labor undertaken by the GOP's Thompsons, crises that everyone agreed were intractable—urban decay, violent crime, family breakdown—seemed, from the vantage point of the millennium, to have been successfully tamed.

In the 1970s and 1980s, conservatives had pushed for stricter sentencing and more prisons; in the 1990s, those same prisons filled up while crime fell precipitously. In the 1970s and 1980s, conservative thinkers from Myron Magnet to Charles Murray had argued that liberal welfare policies hurt the very people they were supposed to be helping. In the 1990s, the Gingrich- and Clinton-crafted, Wisconsin-inspired welfare reform proved to be a boon for the underclass, driving down teen births and moving millions of Americans from dependency to self-sufficiency. For decades, conservatives had argued that free trade and free markets created more wealth than any competing system; by the end of the 1990s, it was hard to find a pundit or politician the world over who disagreed, outside of a few socialist redoubts and protectionist lost colonies.

Conservatives had attacked affirmative action for a generation, but in the 1990s Ward Connerly actually did something about it, pushing a series of ballot initiatives that swept away racial preferences in higher education in over a dozen states. Conservatives had argued for a balanced budget since time immemorial; by the end of the decade they had one, and a surplus besides. As late as 1992, Dan Quayle had been laughed off the political stage for attacking the example set by Murphy Brown's unwed motherhood; by the end of the Clinton years, even many liberals agreed with the *Atlantic Monthly*'s 1995 announcement that "Dan Quayle was right."

It was the decade of what Tom Wolfe called the "Great Re-Learning," the rightward reaction against the dramatic socio-economic and cultural changes wrought by the birth-control pill, the Sexual Revolution, the drug culture, and the movement of women into the workforce. America had experimented with a lifestyle liberalism that shaded into libertinism; now, in the shadow of AIDS and social chaos, the nation stepped back a little way from the precipice. Divorce rates leveled off at last, and even began to fall; the abortion rate dropped for the first time since *Roe v. Wade*; teen births, rising since the 1960s, fell and fell. Teenagers waited longer to have sex; they used drugs less frequently than their parents had and went to church more often. The crack epidemic burned itself out; AIDS was contained if not yet cured. Homosexuality continued its march toward cultural acceptance, but even in the gay community there were conservatizing trends at work as the flamboyance and provocations of the ACT UP era gave way to the marriage movement's campaign for bourgeois respectability.

Not every trend reversed itself: The marriage rate continued to fall, as did the birthrate (only increasing immigration, much of it illegal, kept population growth robust), and the illegitimacy rate continued to climb, until by 2000, 30 percent of white children, and an astonishing 70 percent of black children, were born to single mothers. The falling crime rate was good news, but the drop depended in part on increasingly draconian sentences and an ever-growing archipelago of prisons—and perhaps on the high abortion rates of the 1970s and '80s. And many of the improving social indicators were epiphenomena of the largest economic expansion in forty years, rather than strong indicators of a culture restored to health.

Nonetheless, the 1990s were a great decade in American life, and a great decade, economically at least, for the long-suffering working class. For the first time since the 1970s, the average family income began to climb, and so did the average hourly wage. Things improved for the working poor and the more prosperous working-class voters alike: The poverty rate dropped by a fourth, and families in the middle of the income distribution enjoyed large gains as well. After years of stagnation, the Reaganites' assumption that low taxes and breakneck growth alone would solve the working class's problems seemed to have been vindicated by the wonders of deficit reduction (which, of course, the Reagan administration had never managed to pursue), free markets, and free trade.

The War on Clinton

But it was free-market capitalism filtered through the neoliberal prism of the Clinton administration, and this many conservatives could not abide. After 1994, Clinton ought to have been an ideal partner for the Right; his neoliberalism was to the left of the Republican majority, but it had a great deal in common with the applied neoconservatism of a Giuliani or a Thompson—and not only because it accepted Thompson's Wisconsin program as a model for a national welfare reform. Just as Gingrich had taken Congress by promising accountability in the House and Senate, so too did Clinton pursue a similar agenda to the executive branch, where the Al Gore–led crusade to "reinvent government" did more to streamline the federal behemoth than anything George W. Bush would subsequently attempt. Robert Rubin's free-trading, deficit-conscious economic policy was more left-wing than the supply-siders, but more right-wing than any Democratic Treasury Department had ever been before. And just as Nixon had accepted much of the economic consensus of his era—wage and price controls, Keynesian pump-priming, talk of a guaranteed national income—so Clinton bowed to the national mood and publicly ruled out any further expansions of government power.

Yet just as liberals had hated Nixon, practically to the point of derangement, so many conservatives loathed Clinton. Looking back, this seems difficult to believe—not that the Right opposed Clinton, or even despised him, but that they let their feelings play such havoc with their political good sense. Conservatives had spent the better part of two decades watching as first Nixon and then Reagan and then even the cautious, centrist George H. W. Bush provoked liberals to astonishing outbursts of vitriol, to wild conspiracy theories and whispers of fascism, which only succeeded in alienating them from the much-more-reasonable sentiments of the American public. Yet instead of learning from the opposition's mistakes, conservatives seemed determined to repeat them and take from Clinton the pound of flesh that was owed to them for a generation's worth of liberal outrages, by whatever means were necessary.

Like the Bourbons after Napoleon, they had learned nothing and forgotten nothing, and so the same Right that had long opposed overzealous investigative journalism, congressional fishing expeditions, and loose-cannon independent prosecutors took up the liberals' weapons and left their sense of proportion by the wayside. Clinton was everything they accused him of being—a rake and a cad and a liar, a man whose private promiscuity mirrored his lack of political principle. But while his moral offenses were significant, his legal offenses were ultimately minor league, and no matter how many times Republicans insisted that it was about the law, and not the sex, it was hard to escape the impression that they were trying to refight the battles of the Sexual Revolution on more favorable ground, and this time win them.

If so, they had misjudged the country's mood. America at the close of the twentieth century was a "newly cautious society," as David Frum remarked in *How We Got Here*, his history of the 1970s, but "not a remoralized one"—and for that matter, even the more moralistic 1950s had deliberately papered over its politicians' vices. Once Clinton's conduct was exposed, he ought to have resigned, but using the power of impeachment to enforce a lost principle of masculine honor was an act of quixotic recklessness, and one that cost conservatives dearly.

It cost them popularity, and it cost them seats in 1998, after Newt Gingrich—outflanked by Clinton for the umpteenth time—assured his colleagues that they need only run on the White House's scandal, and that an actual agenda could wait until the dust settled and their majority swelled. Religious conservatives, in particular, overreached their way into a backlash, which left them despairing of the nation's future and talking darkly about withdrawing from the political process entirely—this, in spite of all the cultural ground they had regained since the 1970s. The small-government Right lost an opportunity as well, one that hasn't reappeared since. Years afterward, in 2005, it was revealed that Clinton had been seriously considering pushing Social Security reform in the waning years of his second term, with a proposal that might have included some form of private accounts. A bipartisan compromise that moved the welfare state rightward might have gelled if the Right hadn't spent two years trying, fruitlessly, to wrap a noose around Boy Clinton's neck.

Such a compromise, though, would have required the Right to work with Clinton, which conservatives could never seem to resign themselves to doing. This wasn't just because they resented Clinton's political savvy and his ability to seize a political moment that should by rights have belonged to them; it was also simple revulsion against what Clinton represented, against the '60s generation that had been chastened into Bobo-dom but kept its narcissism and shallowness intact. After feuding with radicals for the better part of a generation, one would have expected conservatives to appreciate rivals who were open to compromises with the Right, who thought the free market was a great thing and who were happy to deregulate industry and streamline government, who could accept welfare reform and chatter about private Social Security accounts. But instead, throughout the Clinton years, conservatives seemed to be nostalgic for their old left-wing antagonists—not only because they were easier to beat, but because they were easier to respect. Sure, the Clinton White House might have been closer to conservatives on matters of policy than many older, leftier Democrats, but that was only *because the Clintonites didn't believe in anything*. To the true believers on the Right, nothing was worse than unbelief.

The Road to Crawford

Inevitably, the more the Republicans defined themselves as the anti-Clinton party, the more their majority eroded, particularly among working-class voters, who didn't much care for Clinton but who liked their rising incomes and who responded favorably when he cast himself as the defender of the old New Deal programs, the M2E2 set (Medicare, Medicaid, Education, and the Environment) that the Gingrich revolutionaries briefly and fatally attempted to scale back. Working-class voters wanted the applied neoconservatism of the Contract with America, they wanted welfare reform and aggressive policing and low taxes, but they didn't want Goldwater-style government-cutting, and they made the GOP pay for contemplating it. After the disastrous government shutdown gambit, the Republicans lost all the battleground states in the Dole-Clinton presidential race and began to shed congressional seats in the Rust Belt and the Pacific Northwest, where white working-class supermajorities had been crucial to Reaganite and Gingrichian success; between 1994 and 1996, non–college-educated voters' support for congressional Democrats increased by 10 percentage points.

Then came the impeachment debacle and the losses of 1998, which turned off working-class voters (particularly Catholics) who didn't share the evangelical zeal of figures like Kenneth Starr. Suddenly the Republican Party seemed in danger of becoming a purely Southern party, identified too strongly with the "folkways of one regional subculture," as Christopher Caldwell warned in an *Atlantic Monthly* essay, and too eager to urge "their imposition on the rest of the country."

On the Democratic side of the aisle, meanwhile, the GOP's blunders and their own party's inroads into the working-class vote suggested the possibility that Fred Dutton's dream, in its neoliberal incarnation, might be on the verge of coming true. In one of the savvier books of the era, *The Emerging Democratic Majority*, Ruy Teixeira and John B. Judis pointed out that so long as Democrats could sustain a substantial amount of working-class support and hold on to their base among minorities and union members, the party's growing edge among the country's professionals—the meritocrats, the Bobos, the mass upper class—seemed to open the possibility of a new realignment, in which the party's lost majority would finally be restored. "George McGovern's revenge," they called it, but the real victory would be Fred Dutton's.

To the wiser heads on the Right, the setbacks of 1996 and 1998 suggested that while conservatism might be ascendant, the conservative movement itself was in need of reinvention. It wasn't just the fruitless War on Clinton: Conservatives were also victims of their own success, and of the Democrats' co-option of Republican ideas. The Right's appeal to working-class voters had been built on crime, welfare, the mismanagement of tax dollars, and the anti-Americanism and foreign-policy weakness of America's liberal elite. Now taxes were low, crime had fallen, welfare had been reformed, the economy was growing, the Cold War was over, and the McGovernites had grown up and become neoliberal and safely bourgeois (the occasional dalliance with an intern aside). All of these developments were conservative triumphs, in a sense, but they also took winning issues off the table, and what remained on the conservative agenda were harder items to sell. Slashing the M2E2 cluster wasn't a political winner in the nineties any more than in the days of Goldwater, and the Right's push for a broader remoralization of society seemed less urgent in an age when crime was falling and the other indicators were pointing up. It was a perilous moment for Republicans, requiring finesse and an air of moderation, rather than Gingrich's rhetorical fusillades or Starr's mix of prurience and Puritanism. It required leaders who, like Reagan and Clinton, could persuade the American people rather than just hector them.

Such leadership was exactly what conservatives suddenly lacked. As the 2000 election approached, then, the Right went out in search of a candidate who embodied conservatism's strengths rather than the GOP's weaknesses. They were looking for a figure untainted by the Republican Congress's unpopularity, a politician who could channel Reagan as well as Gingrich, who could employ the common touch as well as the briefing book. Such a candidate would be a successful governor from a major state, ideally, with a track record of the kind of applied neoconservatism that had made the Republican governors the backbone of the party throughout the 1990s. He would have a record of reaching across the aisle, to defuse the notion that conservatives were just partisan hatchet men, and he would have a record of applying right-wing ideas to traditionally liberal issues—like education, say—and stealing them out from under the Democrats, the better to woo the Sam's Club demographic. He would accept that government couldn't be slashed to the bone immediately, but he would also have a long-range strategy to reduce the public appetite for federal largesse by finding ways to demonstrate the superiority of the private sector. And he would be able to speak the Southern-inflected language of the Religious Right, but also translate it into an ecumenical rhetoric of moral renewal that would charm the religious middle as well.

In Crawford, Texas, there seemed to be such a man.

5

The Age of Bush

Midway through George W. Bush's second term, as the 2006 midterms approached, the *Washington Monthly* asked seven conservatives to explain why they were rooting for a GOP defeat in November. Some of them complained about the Iraq War, some about the Bush administration's expansive view of executive power, some about the GOP's social conservatism. But nearly all of them agreed that the domestic policy failings of the Bush years were primarily a matter of too much spending. The trouble with Bush and his supposedly conservative administration, in other words, was that he governed like a liberal.

This assessment of where the Bush era's domestic policy went wrong has come to be shared by paleoconservatives and libertarians; Phyllis Schlafly and John McCain; Dick Armey and George Will. Bush's fiscal apostasy is perhaps the only evil that Pat Buchanan and Andrew Sullivan have joined hands—rhetorically, at least—to condemn. The next Republican president, the emerging conservative consensus insists, needs to relearn the tenets of the right-wing catechism and renounce the crypto-liberal heresies of the last six years. Only then will the conservative movement return to the broad sunlit uplands it reached, fleetingly, under the leadership of Ronald Reagan and Newt Gingrich.

It's an appealing fantasy, in which ideological purity leads to political success; it's the mirror image, perhaps unsurprisingly, of the liberal fantasy about George W. Bush, in which all his blunders are the inevitable result of too *much* conservatism, not too little. "The truth revealed by the Bush years," the liberal sociologist Alan Wolfe argued in 2006, is that "bad government—indeed, bloated, inefficient, corrupt, and unfair government—is the only kind of conservative government there is." A flood of left-of-center polemics have shared his assessment, insisting that Bush has governed from the "hard right," the "radical right," and that his administration's forays into moderation have been nothing more than stalking horses for cronyism, which is the inevitable result of letting conservatives—who, after all, don't believe in government in the first place—get their hands on the levers of the welfare state. As Noam Scheiber of the *New Republic* put it shortly after Hurricane Katrina, "If you happen to think bureaucracies are structurally incapable of improving people's lives . . . then you have two choices: You can either slash the bureaucracy and refund taxpayers' money, or you can reconcile yourself to the existence of bureaucracy and run it as a patronage operation." Thus "compassionate conservatism" invariably equals Michael Brown, and "big government conservatism" leads inexorably to Jack Abramoff.

The reality, of course, is somewhat more complicated than these two caricatures. Bush *is* a conservative, as the liberals argue, and he *has* been willing to deviate from conservative orthodoxy, as his right-wing critics complain. But neither quality, nor the combination thereof, doomed his administration to Carteresque approval ratings. Bush may be remembered on the left as a crypto-fascist extremist who hijacked American democracy and dragged it rightward, and on the right as a well-meaning crypto-liberal who sold out the legacy of Ronald Reagan, but neither of these images do justice to his distinctive political achievements or to the potential that his administration once held for American life. Observers on both sides of the aisle have soured on Bush, and justly so, but reckoning with his failures shouldn't mean ignoring his successes.

It wasn't just luck, after all, that carried Bush to his strong showing against Al Gore, when every economic indicator suggested that Gore should have clobbered him; or that increased the GOP's advantage in the off-cycle elections of 2002, when the majority party nearly always loses seats; or that sent John Kerry down to defeat in 2004, in spite of plummeting public support for the Iraq War. Bush lost the majority he built, eventually, but he also won more political victories than any right-of-center politician since Ronald Reagan. Conservatives and liberals alike can learn a great deal from what this administration has done wrong, but only if they are also willing to acknowledge the things that it has done right.

The Bush Majority

In September 1999, amid a heated inside-the-Beltway debate over the earned income tax credit, then-candidate George W. Bush spoke out against the congressional GOP's efforts to defer paying the reimbursement to low-income families. "I don't think they ought to balance their budget on the backs of the poor," he argued, adding, "I think we ought to make the tax code such that it's easier for people to move from near poverty to the middle class." A few weeks later, in a speech in New York City, he went further: "Too often," Bush argued, "my party has confused the need for limited government with a disdain for government itself . . . There are human problems that persist in the shadow of affluence."

This stance, one of the first controversial positions he took as a presidential candidate, earned Bush a great deal of criticism from his fellow conservatives. Gary Bauer, then running for president, called the "backs of the poor" statement a "classic Ted Kennedy, Barney Frank, Democratic National Committee line." Rush Limbaugh suggested that Bush had left D.C. Republicans "dying on the congressional battlefield." Paul Weyrich described Bush, with obvious venom, as a "moderate politician."

But Bush's message resonated with the public. For thirty years, the Democrats had struggled to move beyond the self-marginalizing tendencies of their base; in the late 1990s, the Republicans often seemed in danger of falling into the same trap, becoming the party of prudery, don't-tread-on-me nationalism, and an angry antigovernment message that partook more of Ruby Ridge than Reagan. In leading the GOP out of this snare, Bush returned to the animating insight of the post-Goldwater Republican Party: The right can succeed only if it champions a politics of solidarity as well as a politics of liberty.

His critics never liked the way he went about it: Liberal journalists sneered at the phony diversity of the 2000 GOP convention, the gospel choirs and minority speakers; many right-wingers grumbled over Bush's near-obsession with education reform and poverty talk, his "when people are hurting, the government's got to move" rhetoric, and his fascination (or Karl Rove's) with capturing a larger chunk of the Hispanic vote. But these gestures and goals were crucial to restoring the Republican Party's credibility with working-class whites and building up its credibility with working-class blacks and Latinos. They enabled Bush to consolidate the GOP's position as a national party, rather than one defined exclusively by the habits and biases of the now-solidly-Republican South.

He didn't run away from the GOP's Southern heartland, however, a path that John McCain, among others, seemed eager to try, and that was urged on Bush by nearly every "centrist" commentator. Instead, he set out to find the places where Southern folkways and the American mainstream intersect. The War on Terror was the most important catalyst, obviously, because it reminded working-class voters—for the first time since the end of the Cold War—of the disconnect between the Democratic Party's base and the rest of the nation on matters of national security. But it wasn't only 9/11: On domestic policy, too, the language of the Bush years moved conservatives toward the center, and the center toward conservatives, by articulating a vision of politics in which conservative ideas promote not only individual freedom but the common good as well.

This vision owed a great debt to religious conservatives, whom the Bush administration wisely treated as an integral part of the Right's governing coalition, rather than an embarrassing interest group that needed to be kept safely sidelined—the approach of Bob Dole, and to a certain extent Bush's father as well. In the spring of 2000, William Kristol and David Brooks argued in the *Weekly Standard* that John McCain could build on the existing Reagan coalition of economic and social conservatives by explicitly linking religious appeals to patriotic appeals, in the process broadening the call to moral renewal. But this was Bush's strategic goal as well, and one that he was actually better suited to achieve than McCain. Whereas the Arizona senator has always seemed almost physically uncomfortable with the Religious Right, Bush's personal identification with evangelicalism provided credibility for his quest—through faith-based initiatives, say, or the fight against AIDS in Africa, or even the (often-misguided) push for immigration reform—to broaden the GOP's moral agenda beyond its long-running focus on abortion and gay rights.

Indeed, Bush often seemed to appropriate not only the language of conservative Christianity but of liberal Christianity as well, and particularly the left-Catholic notion of a "seamless garment of life" that would encompass issues of wealth and poverty as well as matters of life and death. Bush man-

aged this trick while holding a firmer line on judicial nominations—the central issue in both the abortion and gay marriage
debates—than any Republican president before him. And his
political victories demonstrated that a politician's identification
with religious conservatism need not be a liability in a general
election, as everyone in the media establishment (and many
people in the Republican Party) assumed to be the case. With
an assist from his speechwriters, Bush grasped that the idiom
of American politics is essentially moral and religious, and that
the increasing secularization of the Democratic Party offered
the GOP a chance to occupy the religious and political mainstream for a generation to come.

But Bush's vision owed its greatest debt to Nixon. By now,
it's become conventional wisdom that the Bush White House
resembles the Nixon White House more than any other, and
the comparison is deployed, without fail, as a term of abuse.
But just as Nixon crafted a new ideological synthesis that made
working-class conservatism viable in the first place, Bush re-
invented the Nixon coalition for a new millennium and attempted to succeed where Nixon failed—by making the Republican Party responsive to the economic concerns of the working
class, the Sam's Club voters who had swung back and forth between the two parties for thirty years, and by expanding the
GOP's appeal beyond working-class whites to Hispanics and
blacks as well.

Bush didn't just point out the link between permissiveness
and poverty, for instance, as conservatives had been doing for
years; he proposed actually doing something about it, the way
his fellow governors had done in the 1990s, building on the
successes of welfare reform while attacking small-government
conservatives for their eagerness to sacrifice even those anti-
poverty programs (like the earned income tax credit) that actually worked. Where McCain's conservative reformism promoted
the pet causes of the media and the Boboized upper-middle

class—campaign finance reform, antitobacco legislation, global warming—Bush emphasized education, the issue at the core of working-class struggles in a globalized age. In both cases, accountability was to be the watchword: private-public partnerships to help the less fortunate climb toward self-sufficiency, rather than unresponsive bureaucracies; higher standards for public schools and increased funding for private experiments in education, rather than tax dollars poured away in vain on failing institutions.

On size-of-government questions, meanwhile, as Jonathan Rauch argued in 2003, Bush's insight was to shift conservatism's focus and to attempt an end run around the roadblocks that had stopped Gingrich and Reagan's government-cutting crusades in their tracks. Rather than focus on the "supply side" of government, or the amount of government spending—the place where the 1994 "revolutionaries" had run up against a wall of working-class support for the M2E2 cluster—he focused on the "demand side," or the need for government services. Thus marriage promotion would foster stable two-parent families and diminish demand for welfare services. Child tax credits would make it easier for working-class parents to get by and for working-class children to thrive. Dividend tax cuts would reward the thrift and financial independence of a growing "investor class," while helping to build a self-sufficient "ownership society" in which the goods of American life were widely dispersed. Other proposals would provide the poor and the working class with capital endowments for job training, purchasing a home, and starting a business. The plan was that such measures would, over time, deliver a lasting working-class majority by "changing the incentives of politics," as Ken Mehlman put it, in the same way that the New Deal did in the 1930s.

It worked, for a time—or at least the message won votes, even if its execution left much to be desired. Under Bush's leadership, the Republican Party's losses in the 1990s were reversed:

Working-class Perot voters returned to the fold, the gender gap began to close, Hispanics voted for the GOP in numbers not seen since Reagan, and there were even hints that the party might be making inroads among African Americans. The result, by the 2004 election, was a Republican Party more Middle American than ever before—the party of optimists and entrepreneurs and investors, as in every election since Goldwater and before, but also the party of churchgoers, who broke for the GOP in record numbers, and the party of families with children, whose turn to the Right created a "baby gap" that threatened to leave the Democrats in the demographic dust.

Above all, it was the party of Sam's Club—not only the working-class men who had stuck close to the GOP even during the losses of the late 1990s, but working-class women as well. In 2000, when Bush beat Gore (well, almost), he won the votes of white working-class men by 29 percent, up from 8 percent for Bob Dole, but enjoyed only a 7-point advantage among female voters in the Sam's Club demographic. By 2004, his advantage among white working-class women had widened to eighteen points. The pundits dubbed these voters "security moms," hypothesizing that the influence of 9/11 had moved them rightward. This was doubtless true, but while Bush enjoyed a massive advantage among these voters on the question of who could better handle terrorism, he enjoyed a comparable advantage on economic issues as well. Asked which candidate could better steward the economy, white working-class voters preferred Bush to Kerry by 55 percent to 39 percent. In exurbs and office parks, the message of compassionate conservatism had done its work, convincing voters with high-school diplomas or "some college," as the term went, to back the GOP by margins not seen since Reagan and the sweep of 1992.

Such working-class supermajorities were necessary because in an age of rising affluence and falling crime, many voters from the Nixon-Reagan majority were trending leftward, as their lifestyles pulled them up and away from Middle America, into the quasi-European comforts of the coastal states. Voters who were once flinty Rockefeller Republicans and pocketbook-conscious Orange County conservatives were becoming prosperous rentiers, wooed leftward by lifestyle politics to join Judis and Teixeira's emerging Democratic majority and bring Fred Dutton's dream to fruition at last.

But their day was postponed, because for every lost Santa Barbara suburbanite, Bush won a middle-income Latino; for every ex-Republican stockbroker working on his third wife, he captured a socially conservative white Catholic. He lost Connecticut but won New Mexico; lost California but made inroads into the Old Northwest, taking Iowa and coming close in Wisconsin and Minnesota. The heirs of Nelson Rockefeller might be trending Democratic, but Bush found a way to pick off the sons of Cesar Chavez, Hubert Humphrey, and Robert La Follette. If there is a conservative majority in a decade, it will resemble the one that was forged over the past six years, and it will owe a debt to the political skill of George W. Bush.

What Bush Did Wrong

But as with Nixon, the larger project—a conservatism attuned to the needs of working-class voters—has been deferred. There is blame enough to go around, from a blundering Republican leadership in the House and Senate, to a Democratic Party that decided midway through the Bush years to stop working with the administration and start obstructing it (which proved a savvy move on their part), to a media that briefly glorified Bush's foreign policy but was always quick to trash his domestic initiatives. And there were institutional and ideological barriers as well, to the kind of pro-government conservatism that Bush attempted to implement. The liberal critique was proven right, at least up to a point: Many honest small-government conservatives weren't interested in overseeing programs that they would prefer to see slashed or abolished, and so their place was filled, in the Bush years, by an assortment of cynical operators for whom the only guiding principle was to keep Republicans (and themselves) fat, happy, and securely in power.

Ultimately, though, the buck stops with Bush himself, who articulated a vision of a working-class conservatism but failed to follow through. He started promisingly enough: No Child Left Behind, for all its myriad faults, could have been a building block of a domestic policy that risked conservative wrath in order to co-opt Democratic issues and constituencies, accepting increased spending in order to inject higher standards, greater accountability, and even some free-market mechanisms into a sclerotic bureaucracy. But from 2001 on, Bush seemed to lose both his interest in policy detail and his willingness to fight battles with the interest groups in his own party. What remained was the rhetoric, the narrative of politics, which was enough to build a majority but not enough to keep it.

You can blame some of this drift on 9/11 and the wars that followed. David Frum has recounted being summoned to a meeting of speechwriters late in 2001, when Bush made it clear that, temporarily at least, "there was no more domestic agenda. The domestic agenda was the same as the foreign agenda: Win the war—then we'll see." But it's also worth considering Bush's past experiences of failure—as a governor and then as a presidential candidate—and the role they may have played in derailing his reformist instincts. As a presidential son, he watched his father get pilloried on the Right for breaking his "no new taxes" pledge, and vowed never to make the same mistake. As governor of Texas, he watched his most ambitious gambit—a proposal to ensure a more equitable distribution of school funding in Texas—get defeated by antitax conservatives in the state senate, who (despite all evidence to the contrary) insisted that shifting the tax burden from homeowners to businesses would represent a tax hike. In each case, the lesson was clear: A GOP politician crossed the party's antitax activists at his peril.

As a presidential candidate, Bush faced a similar moment of political truth. During the long run-up to the 2000 presidential campaign, the Bush camp assumed that they'd face a formidable movement-conservative challenger. Steve Forbes—now remembered, if at all, as a footnote from the campaign—was viewed as a serious threat, thanks to his bank account and the support of conservative veterans like Weyrich and Richard Viguerie. But instead, Bush faced an unexpected challenge from the *left*. The irony of John McCain's insurgency in 2000 is that it drew precisely on the theme of a reinvigorated citizenship that had briefly been Bush's exclusive territory, and demonstrated the wide appeal of a conservative politics that promised to do more than "leave us alone." And so, in a strange turn of events, Bush was forced to confront not a doctrinaire, narrow conservatism in the form of Steve Forbes, but rather his own mirror image.

Bush struck back, in part, by emphasizing his reformist bona fides—selling himself as a "reformer with results," a much-ridiculed slogan that actually made an accurate contrast with McCain's relatively undistinguished policymaking career to that point. But he also fell back on the conservative status quo and cast himself as the candidate of the doctrinaire Right, emphasizing a sweeping tax cut and not much else. The intellectual spadework of Bush's years in Austin was abandoned in the heat of the campaign, as the candidate and his surrogates blasted McCain as a liberal and relied on right-wing machine politics (complete with dirty tricks and smear campaigns) to bring him down. After stinging defeats in the South and West, McCain retreated from the scene, but not before shifting George W. Bush's image—and perhaps his self-image—toward an unimaginative ideological orthodoxy.

He would tack back toward the center in the general election, of course. The pre-McCain Bush reasserted himself, as did Karl Rove's theory that this could be a realigning moment—like the election of William McKinley in 1896, he liked to say. But then the 2000 election itself turned out to be far closer than Rove had anticipated—perhaps, post-election polls suggested, because there weren't as many swing voters as he had thought. Here's how Thomas Edsall tells the story in his *Building Red America*:

> In late 2000, even as the result of the presidential election was still being contested in court, George W. Bush's chief pollster Matt Dowd was writing a memo for Rove that would reach a surprising conclusion. Based on a detailed examination of poll data from the previous two decades, Dowd's memo argued that the percentage of swing voters had shrunk to a tiny fraction of the electorate. Most self-described "independent" voters "are independent in name only," Dowd told me in an interview describing his memo. "Seventy-five percent of independents vote straight ticket" for one party or the other. Once such independents are reclassified as Democrats or Republicans, a key trend emerges: Between 1980 and 2000, the percentage of *true* swing voters fell from a very substantial 24 percent of the electorate to just 6 percent. In other words, the center was literally disappearing. Which meant that, instead of having every incentive to govern as "a uniter, not a divider," Bush now had every reason to govern via polarization.

There are reasons to be suspicious of this tale, not least because it's hard to imagine a political mind as subtle as Karl Rove's buying into it wholeheartedly. The Dowd theory was superficially flawed because even a 6 percent swing in a fifty-fifty nation is a huge, majority-making shift, as the next three election cycles would demonstrate. It was deeply flawed because great politicians don't just respond to the electorate, they actively shape it, and by embarking on a strategy of "polarization" a president forfeits his chance at political greatness.

Nevertheless, the Dowd memo's possible influence over Rove, and by extension Bush, helps explain the weird schizophrenia that would characterize the administration's domestic policy, which oscillated between a "base" strategy and a "realignment" strategy and never seemed to consider how the two contradicted each other. Thus the first term would be shaped by sweeping, across-the-board tax cuts, because that was what the party's activists wanted—tax cuts in peace and war, in surplus and deficit alike. Their benefits were murky: Reagan had cut taxes in a country groaning under its tax burden and rife with tax revolts; Bush cut them at a time when voters put tax relief far down their list of priorities. (It's worth noting that while Bush substantially increased his share of the vote from 2000 to 2004, the "investor class," beloved of supply-siders, cast the same proportion of its votes for him in both elections, in spite of all the money he saved them.) And their downside was obvious: When joined to wartime spending, they provided easy fodder for accusations of fiscal irresponsibility.

As a result, there was little money left over for the kind of realigning, "compassionate-conservative" agenda that Bush had promoted in the campaign. A massive new prescription drugs benefit for seniors was passed in spite of the deficits, and its market mechanisms turned out to work better than both liberal and conservative critics expected. But the tax cuts helped ensure that the rest of Bush's programs were underfunded—from No Child Left Behind to the kind of small-bore antipoverty initiatives that he had championed in the campaign. (Two of the most cutting accounts of Bush administration ineptitude came from John Dilulio and David Kuo, both of the faith-based initiatives office.) Education and poverty received administration attention only when political expediency demanded it: Once Hurricane

Katrina put the issues in the public eye, there was a swift and transparently cynical attempt to minimize the political damage by throwing New Deal–style money at the Gulf region.

The same pattern played itself out when he spent his much-ballyhooed "political capital" on a push to dramatically reshape Social Security—again, a pet issue of conservative activists—rather than, say, an attempt at health-care reform or tax reform, which was what the country, and particularly the working class, wanted. There were genuinely good ideas buried in Bush's ill-defined war on the Social Security status quo, but it was at once opaque and threatening to many working-class Americans, and like Bill Clinton's health-care plan in 1993, it was defeated without a vote being cast. And while the tax cuts had been misguided in certain respects, at least they had passed and offered a kick start to a flagging economy in the process. The Social Security debacle, on the other hand, didn't just end in defeat; it transformed George W. Bush into a domestic policy lame duck.

Of course, Bush's Nixonian project might have been doomed anyway by the abiding incompetence of his administration. Dilulio, in much-publicized first-term remarks to the journalist Ron Suskind, dismissed Bush's advisers as "Mayberry Machiavellis," while Frum, in his otherwise admiring portrait of Bush's first three years, remarked that "one seldom heard an unexpected thought in the Bush White House or met someone who possessed unusual knowledge . . . conspicuous intelligence seemed actively unwelcome." Too often, the White House seemed to repeat the mistakes of post–Great Society liberalism, tailoring its agenda to specific interest groups—dividend tax cuts for investors, steel tariffs for blue-collar swing voters in Ohio, immigration reform for Hispanics, gay marriage for the Christian Right—rather than designing a reform agenda that spoke, as the best of Bush's rhetoric did, to the nation as a whole. And too often, its policies were associated with hacks and cronies and incompetents, figures like Rod Paige and Harriet Miers and Alberto Gonzales, who seemed to have been promoted above their pay grade because of a personal connection to the president.

Over time, these two overlapping flaws—a team with a better grasp of politics than policy and a White House that prized loyalty over brilliance—bore fruit in the bills the administration signed into law. For instance, the country could have used an energy initiative that either addressed Sam's Club voters' concerns over rising prices at the pump or accepted short-term pain in an effort to break what Bush (accurately enough) termed America's "addiction to oil." Instead, it got an expensive package of handouts to oil and natural-gas interests, more or less written by energy lobbyists, that did neither. The country could have used a sensible immigration reform that predicated a path to citizenship for aliens already here in a serious attempt to take control of the borders, reduce lawlessness, and control the inflow of low-skilled labor. Instead, Bush ended up championing a proposal that embodied the worst qualities of McCainism—it flattered the president's moral vanity and won plaudits from the press, propped up the upper-middle class at the expense of the working class, and alienated his base into the bargain. The country could have used a renewed focus on its transportation infrastructure; instead, it got a ridiculously expensive highway bill most famous for its "bridge to nowhere."

For a time after 9/11, of course, none of this seemed to matter, since foreign policy appeared to offer a chance to secure the Bush majority without worrying about the contradictions that bedeviled the administration's domestic policy. For the first time since Reagan, the full force of the GOP's advantage on national security was brought to bear against a Democratic Party whose pacifist fringe was actually larger, in numbers if not in clout, than in the early 1970s. It was the Cold War all over again, except that 9/11 was far more immediately traumatic and promised perhaps even greater dividends for the party that was associated with a robust foreign-policy response. Bush's approval ratings went sky high, his support among working-class voters rose through the roof, and polls showed that even twentysomethings, usually a liberal constituency, were leaning Republican in significant numbers. The Rove realignment was within the party's grasp, or so it briefly seemed, and without all those pesky domestic compromises cluttering it up.

Of course, once the Iraq War turned sour—thanks to mismanagement that was of a piece with the Bush administration's domestic stumblings—the ties that bound this majority together began to fray. Having failed to follow through on a reformist agenda when his popularity was at its peak, Bush was forced to fall back on fear—of terrorists and of liberals—to keep his party's hold on power, and it wasn't enough. And the danger to the GOP was greater than it had been during previous trips into the political wilderness. Both Clinton and Carter, for instance, had beaten Republicans by downplaying foreign policy and thereby minimizing the GOP's advantage in that arena. But the advantage endured, in the seventies and nineties alike, waiting only for a moment like the Iran hostage crisis or 9/11 to come to the fore again. Whereas Bush's failure in Iraq didn't just negate the Republican foreign-policy advantage in the short run, it threatened to break the GOP's long-term reputation as the policy of competence and strength abroad.

Without an edge in foreign policy, all the GOP's pre-Bush problems reasserted themselves. Bush's success at softening the Religious Right's harder edges slipped away as the GOP drifted, and in its place there were provocations like the Terri Schiavo fiasco, which turned off the religious middle. The domestic policy issues of the Nixon and Reagan eras weren't resonant anymore: Crime was still low, affirmative action and taxes were no longer pressing concerns, and on immigration, the party was torn between two laudable objectives—increasing its appeal among Hispanics and addressing working-class concern about rising disorder and growing inequality. The outlines of Bushism were broadly popular, but the specifics were increasingly unattractive, and as David Brooks wrote late in 2006, the "G.O.P. has become like a company with a great mission statement, but no domestic policy products to sell."

Worse, the socioeconomic trends of the 1970s and 1980s were reasserting themselves. The working-class problems that had persisted in the Clinton-Gingrich golden age—high illegitimacy and divorce rates, and increasing economic insecurity amid general prosperity—endured under Bush as well, while the indicators that had turned up in the Clinton years slipped southward once more. The economy recovered relatively swiftly after the stock market bubble collapsed and the twin towers fell, but while the broad indicators—growth, productivity growth, and unemployment—were favorable, the working class was getting left behind again. The median income stagnated, the average hourly wage declined, and inequality increased. Wealth was being created at a breakneck pace, but it fell into fewer and fewer hands—not just the top 10 or 25 percent this time, but the top 1 percent, the CEOs and hedge fund managers, a trend ripe for populist backlash.

Republicans complained about a "Dangerfield economy," which got no respect from voters and the (liberal) press, but they were missing the point. As the *New Republic*'s Jon Chait put it, "fast economic growth, after all, is a means to an end— namely, higher living standards for most people. By any decent moral calculation, an economy that does not produce higher living standards for most people is not a good one." The Bush economy—and by extension, Bush's entire domestic policy— wasn't delivering, particularly for the Sam's Club voters who had given the Republicans their majority. Once again, conservatives had promised to lead working-class America out of its post-seventies struggles. Once again, they had failed.

The Return of the Democrats

The moment was tailor made for the opposition party, and the Democrats finally delivered. After years of being pilloried as ineffectual losers, usually by their own coreligionists in the press, they ran the savviest campaign they had managed since 1992. On foreign policy, they ran against Bush's incompetence, using hawkish figures like John Murtha and James Webb to hammer the president for bleeding America dry in a futile war and keeping the party's Michael Moores and Jimmy Carters safely offstage until it was all over. They managed the difficult trick of convincing voters that they would get the troops out of Iraq more or less immediately without actually coming out and *saying* it, which would have ensured that the GOP's "cut and run" arrows hit their mark.

On cultural issues, meanwhile, Democrats turned their long-running disadvantages into an unexpected strength. After 2004, liberalism was divided between those convinced that they needed to reach out to churchgoers and those who were persuaded that the mixture of religion and politics represented an existential threat to the American republic. This division could have weakened the party, but instead the Democrats used it to pull off two parallel campaigns in the run-up to '06. On the one hand, Democratic strategists and candidates reached out to religious voters in the Midwest and the Border South, making a play for the churchgoing vote that bolstered candidates like Ted Strickland in Ohio and Heath Shuler in North Carolina. At the same time, left-wing authors and pundits and bloggers kept up a steady stream of books and essays and pamphlets warning of the looming theocratic menace, which stoked the fears of the secular and mildly religious voters who were trending Democratic already, and delivered the party its largest majority ever among the faithless. The result was a coalition that found strength in its own fault lines, making inroads among *both* churchgoers and secularists on the way to its midterm sweep.

This targeted cultural conservatism was joined to a full-throated economic populism that played directly on working-class insecurity. The "Lou Dobbs Democrats," as Jacob Weisberg dubbed them, were demagogic on free trade and talked like conservative Republicans on immigration. They put minimum-wage increases on the ballot in six states, all of them won by Bush in 2004, and the initiatives passed in all six; meanwhile, their candidates argued that the "middle class is being forced into poverty," in the words of Montana's Jon Tester. Their rhetoric included everything but the kitchen sink: It linked Jack Abramoff to Michael Brown to Ken Lay; rising CEO salaries to the Bush tax cuts to oil company profits; the Dubai ports fiasco to the unsecured Mexican border to the debacle in Iraq. And the message worked: Among voters without college degrees, support for congressional Republicans collapsed from 51 percent in 2004 to 43 percent, one of the largest drops in any major demographic category.

It worked for one election cycle, at least. Whether it can deliver in the long run remains to be seen. Liberalism's preferred solution to working-class insecurity—making America more like Europe through a vast expansion of the tax-and-transfer state—is still unpopular with most voters, which is why Democrats talked up economic security in 2006 but were thin on policy detail. To working-class Americans struggling to figure out how to get ahead in a more competitive economy, the Lou Dobbs Democrats don't have much to offer—a minimum wage increase, a critique of the alleged inequities of small-bore trade deals, and tough talk on border security that will be drowned out in a caucus that's eager to liberalize immigration laws and increase the influx of low-skilled laborers. Once the artfully named bills pass and the signing ceremonies finish, working-class voters will probably wonder, as Walter Mondale once put it, "Where's the beef?"

The Right isn't exactly well positioned to profit from their disappointment, however. As the Bush era limps to a close, the GOP is in disarray, and the various conservative factions are at one another's throats, each convinced that if the president had only listened to *them*, everything would have turned out better. As of this writing, the main prescription being urged on Republican leaders by the right-wing intelligentsia is government-cutting and fiscal austerity—the sort of unelectable fidelity to principle that doomed Goldwater in 1964 and Gingrich thirty years later.

Cooler heads in the party will probably prevail, as will political reality. But even if the GOP finds a way to build on Bush's successes rather than abandoning them, his failures are still likely to drag at his successors—particularly the foreign-policy legacy of the Iraq War, which will likely be an albatross for Republicans for many years to come.

As for Bush himself, his legacy is ultimately Nixonian in the worst sense—a record of temporary successes, half-grasped achievements, and squandered opportunities. There may yet be a lasting right-of-center majority waiting to be built on the political successes of the last six years, but Bush wasn't the leader to do it. He will leave behind an America stuck where it has been for the past two decades—a fifty-fifty nation, waiting for a new majority to emerge. For him, one can already sense history's verdict: a gifted political storyteller who didn't make his story a reality and a leader who brought his party to the edge of the Promised Land, but couldn't guide them in.

For conservatism as a whole, meanwhile, the Bush years represented the best opportunity to come of age as a governing movement—to think seriously about the design of the welfare state, to seize the initiative from its liberal architects, and to find new ways to deliver essential services while building, rather than degrading, the capacity for self-reliance. That opportunity has been wasted. The blame lies largely with Bush himself, but it also lies with a conservative movement that has been unwilling to tailor its thinking to the problems facing its constituents in working-class America and the scope of the challenges ahead.

PART II

THE PARTY OF SAM'S CLUB

6

What's the Matter with the Working Class?

5 1% of Women Are Now Living Without Spouse" ran the headline in the *New York Times* early in 2007. It was the first time in the history of the U.S. Census that more women reported living without a man than with one, and the *Times* reporter used the milestone as an opportunity to celebrate female independence and empowerment and implicitly consign the old "Ozzie and Harriet" model of marriage to the dustbin of history. The story quoted William Frey, a Brookings Institution demographer, who called the shift the "culmination of post-1960 trends associated with greater independence and more flexible lifestyles for women." It quoted Stephanie Coontz, a historian of marriage, who called the dramatic half-century shift—in 1950, just 35 percent of women lacked a spouse—a sign that there was "no going back to a world where we can assume that marriage is the main institution that organizes people's lives." It talked about young people who were delaying marriage. Like "Emily Zuzik, a 32-year-old musician and model who lives in the East Village of Manhattan," or Besse Gardner, twenty-four, who lives with her boyfriend because "they found a great apartment on the beach in Los Angeles" and doesn't "see living to-

gether as an end or even for the rest of our lives—it's just fun right now." It lavished particular attention on older women who had never married or had divorced and were now "delighting in their newfound freedom."

There was, for instance, Shelley Fidler, fifty-nine, a public policy adviser at a mid-Atlantic law firm who has "sworn off marriage" and who "moved from rural Virginia to the vibrant Adams Morgan neighborhood of Washington, D.C., when her 30-year marriage ended." There was Linda Barth, a fifty-six-year-old magazine editor in Houston, and forty-five-year-old Sheila Jamison, "who also lives in the East Village and works for a media company"—both unmarried and both perfectly happy about it. There was Elissa B. Terris, fifty-nine, of Marietta, Georgia, who divorced in 2005 and is returning to college to get a master's degree, taking photography classes, and auditioning for a play. She recently turned down a marriage proposal—because, she said, "I'm just beginning to fly again, I'm just beginning to be me."

It was left to others—David Brooks, the op-ed page's lone conservative, and then Kate Zernike, writing in the Week in Review section a few days later—to throw a little cold water on all this happy news for American women. Both pointed out that most of the country's unmarried women aren't gay divorcées or hard-charging working girls but "less-educated manicurists or housekeepers," in Zernike's example—women, that is, "who might arguably be less able to live on their own." Both Brooks and Zernike noted that many of these women want to get married but delay wedlock until they attain a level of financial stability that, paradoxically, only marriage itself is likely to provide. Zernike pointed out that men of every social class are reliably commitment-phobic during their twenties, but that well-educated men are much more likely to eventually settle down, while working-class men are more likely to effectively "remain boys indefinitely." Brooks noted that "nearly 90 percent of the people who are living together when their child is born plan to get married someday . . . but the vast majority never will."

It was the breezy news story, though, not the more serious follow-ups, that's characteristic of how the current American consensus ignores, misunderstands, or glosses over the nature of the working class's present difficulties. The *Times* is an elite newspaper, written for the rich and the upper-middle class—not only in New York but around the country—and within that world, the conventional wisdom about working-class struggles begins and ends with income. There is an intellectual understanding, among the members of America's leadership class, that American life is increasingly stratified, that the kind of people who read the *Times* are doing far better than those who read the *Post* or the *Daily News* or no newspaper at all. But when *Times* readers look for culprits, they tend to begin with corporate corruption and end with the Republican Party's tax cuts. They're unlikely to push through the figures on stagnating wages, exploding CEO bonuses, and the shrinking middle class to reach the nub of the problem and the place where any serious analysis of working-class anxiety needs to begin—with the domestic sphere and the decline of the working-class family.

The Marriage Gap

The most important thing to understand about today's stratification—economic, social, and cultural—is that it starts at home, where working-class Americans are far less likely than their better-educated peers to enjoy the benefits that flow from stable families. In the fifties, as we have seen, marriage rates, divorce rates, and illegitimacy varied only a little by class and education. In the seventies, that began to change—imperceptibly at first, and then dramatically. The divorce rate exploded across all classes in the late 1960s, but among the college educated it leveled off quickly and then began to drop. In the period from

1970 to '74, 24 percent of all first marriages among Americans with college degrees ended in divorce within ten years; two decades later, that figure had fallen to just 17 percent. During the same period, by contrast, the divorced-within-ten-years rate crept *up* among Americans without a college degree, from 34 to 36 percent. As late as 1980, the divorce rate for women without a four-year college degree was just three percentage points higher than the divorce rate for women with a four-year degree; by 2000, this "divorce divide" stood at nine percentage points.

As with divorce, so with illegitimacy. In 1965, Lyndon Johnson would cite the Moynihan Report's declaration that the black family was in "crisis," with 25 percent of black children born out of wedlock, as the justification for a sweeping "War on Poverty." Forty years later, the illegitimacy rate for non-Hispanic whites matched the black illegitimacy rate of 1965; among Hispanics, whose birthrate is surging, the illegitimacy rate is 45 percent; and among African Americans, almost 70 percent of children are born out of wedlock. More important, this across-the-board increase is better understood in terms of class than race. In the early 1960s, the rate of out-of-wedlock births was 5 percent among the best-educated third of the population and just 7 percent among the least-educated third. Over the next forty years, the illegitimacy rate would triple for the least-educated third, while barely budging among the best-educated segment of the population.

Typically, the rise of out-of-wedlock births is understood as part of the problem of the so-called "underclass"—people trapped in inner-city squalor or rural poverty. But the scope of illegitimacy means that it's now an issue for the broader working class, not just the poorest parts of the non–college-educated population. As Heather Mac Donald noted recently, in the Hispanic population out-of-wedlock childbearing is as common among "churchgoing, blue-collar workers" as it is among the desperately poor. She cites the example of "fifty-year-old Irma and her husband, Rafael," who live in Southern California and who migrated legally from Mexico in the early 1970s:

> Rafael works in a meatpacking plant in Brea; they have raised five husky boys who attend church with them. Yet Irma's sister—a homemaker like herself, also married to a factory hand—is now the grandmother of two illegitimate children, one by each daughter. "I saw nothing in the way my sister and her husband raised her children to explain it," Irma says. "She gave them everything." One of the fathers of Irma's young nieces has four other children by a variety of different mothers. His construction wages are being garnished for child support, but he is otherwise not involved in raising his children.

Where do these tendencies come from? In her invaluable book on the stratification of family life, *Marriage and Caste in America*, Kay Hymowitz points out the paradox of the Sexual Revolution—namely, that the very women who have benefited the most from their newfound freedoms, the well-off and well educated, are also the most likely to embrace the kind of bourgeois lifestyle that predominated before the birth control pill changed the world forever. It's not *exactly* the same, of course; they're more likely to have sex and cohabit before marriage than their mothers were, more likely to delay childbearing into their thirties, and more likely to stop at one or two children rather than pushing on to three or four. But at a fundamental level, they're accepting a conservative understanding of what marriage is and ought to be—a lifelong commitment that predates childbearing and exists in large part for the benefit of the children.

They do so, Hymowitz argues, out of the abiding practicality that has defined upper-middle-class life in America ever since the sixties ran out of steam. "Educated middle-class mothers," she writes, "tend to be dedicated to the Mission—the careful nurturing of their children's cognitive, emotional, and social development, which, if all goes according to plan, will lead to the honor roll and a spot on the debate team, which will in turn lead to a good college, then . . . eventually to a fulfilling career, a big house in a posh suburb, and a sense of meaningful accomplishment." Ideologically, they may believe that marriage should be optional, just one lifestyle choice among many; they accept adultery in their politicians and unwed motherhood from their movie stars; and they have no interest in anything so harsh as bringing back the stigma that used to apply to illegitimacy, divorce, and cohabitation. But "like high-status women since status began, they are preparing their offspring to carry on their way of life," and an old-fashioned marriage offers as good a guarantee of stability and prosperity as you're likely to get.

Working-class women, on the other hand, may actually be more idealistic about marriage, in a sense. But this means that they tend to either rush into impulsive unions that don't end well or place marriage on a pedestal, often putting it off till after they've had children with a man they love but may not quite trust to provide for them permanently. (In a more skill-based economy—more on that below—the typical working-class man isn't as good a catch as he was in the age of lifetime employment.) As Kathryn Edin and Andrew Cherlin have argued, these women often regard marriage as the capstone, rather than the foundation, of family life. And this, in turn, creates a sexual climate in which nobody—not women, not men, not grandparents, and not even children—quite understands what their obligations are, in which a pervasive mistrust clouds every relationship. Women feel used for sex by men who don't want to get married; men feel used for money, "valued only for their not-so-deep pockets," as Hymowitz puts it.

All of this instability is intimately linked to both emotional and economic stress. It's hopefully unnecessary to rehearse a generation's worth of social science on the effects of illegitimacy and divorce. Pick a social indicator, and you'll find that parents and children alike do far better in stable families, even controlling for a host of competing demographic factors. Married men have significantly longer life expectancies than single men and significantly higher incomes. Married women have lower rates of depression than single women, while both single and divorced women are four to five times more likely to be victims of violent crime than their married counterparts. Divorced women are considerably more likely to slip into poverty than their married counterparts, not least because it takes 56 percent more annual income to support two people living apart than it does to support them if they live together.

As with parents, so with children. There are the emotional costs of family instability: Children of divorced parents, a recent study found, are seven times likelier to report feelings of isolation than are children from intact families, three times more likely to say that they felt like "an outsider" in their own home, and only half as likely to say that they "generally felt emotionally safe" during their childhood. They are twice as likely to have poor relationships with their mothers and fathers, to seek psychological counseling, and to get divorced themselves later in life.

Then there are the direct economic consequences: Had family structure remained unchanged from 1970 to 1998, Adam Thomas and Isabel Sawhill recently argued, the late-1990s child poverty rate would have been 13.9 percent, rather than 18.3 percent—which over decades represents millions of lives unscarred by poverty and millions of children more likely to become productive, law-abiding citizens. There are the sociological consequences: Children of single parents tend to have sex too young, marry too young, get pregnant too young, and have children out of wedlock. They are more likely to drop out of high school, less likely to attend college, and more likely to go on welfare, use drugs, or turn to crime. Men raised in a single-parent home are twice as likely to have spent time in jail by their early thirties, even when controlling for a host of other demographic factors, and the percentage of fatherless households in a neighborhood closely tracks with the neighborhood's crime rate.

Critics of efforts to strengthen marriage—and even at this late date, they do exist—often point out that Sweden has twice as many nonmarital births as the United States, and yet Swedish children encounter far less hardship than their American counterparts. But "unmarried" Swedes are actually far more likely to raise their children together than are Americans. From 1900 to 1970, only about 25 percent of American children aged sixteen did not live with both biological parents. As of the 1990s, only half of children *did*. In Sweden, that citadel of sexual laissez-faire, two-thirds of children at fifteen live with both parents. (Indeed, it's worth considering the extent to which this very different European family structure, which more closely resembles America's family structure at midcentury than does our own, accounts for the significant gap in child poverty rates between Europe and America, which is often attributed to generous European welfare states. But this would mean that American conservatives, in turn, ought to acknowledge that generous benefits for mothers and children have not everywhere and always led to family breakdown.) Contrary to well-rehearsed claims of American prudishness, the atomized American family has arguably taken the Sexual Revolution further than the supposedly libertine Swedes.

Moreover, whatever it is that makes cohabitation a semisuccessful substitute for marriage in Scandinavia doesn't exist in the United States. The number of cohabiting couples rose tenfold from 1960 to 2000, and today roughly 10 million Americans are living together outside of wedlock; as with marriage and illegitimacy, there's an inverse relationship between your education level and your likelihood of cohabitation. As a recent study from the Institute for American Values points out, American "adults who live together but do not marry . . . are more similar to singles than to married couples in terms of physical health and disability, emotional well-being and mental health, as well as assets and earnings. Their children more closely resemble the children of single people than the children of married people." Hymowitz notes that research shows that even when a cohabiting couple resembles a married pair in their education levels and income, "they experience more material hardship . . . and get less help from extended families when they do." Meanwhile, remarriage after divorce, while it can improve the life of parents, may be even worse for children than persisting in a stable single-parent household. Children with stepparents are more likely to be abused, both physically and sexually, and less likely to receive the kind of emotional and financial support that they would receive from biological parents. Overall, they resemble the children of single-parent households more than they do kids whose parents' marriage remains intact.

On nearly every front, this "marriage gap" (and the divorce, illegitimacy, and cohabitation gaps) between the well educated and less educated breeds social stratification and economic inequality, by saddling working-class Americans with a host of burdens that their better-educated fellow citizens don't have to bear. You can quantify the results: Gary Burtless of the Brookings Institution estimates that the combination of working-class illegitimacy and assortative marriage in the upper-middle class—the well-off marrying the well-off, closing off the possibility of advancement through marriage—may be responsible for over 30 percent of the growth in income inequality between 1979 and 1996. And you don't have to look at income: Just compare the divorce rate for the parents of Ivy Leaguers, which hovers around just 10 percent, to the divorce rate for the population as a whole. The disparity isn't a coincidence.

Given the impact of familial dissolution on the working class's prospects, then, the oft-heard talking point that social conservatism represents an attempt to distract working-class voters from their "real" concerns dramatically misses the point. Indeed, social conservatism, with its emphasis on stable, traditional families, is a perfectly rational response to the economic consequences of atomization. Liberal pundits get a great deal of mileage out of the fact that the so-called Red states, in spite of their piety and social conservatism, have higher rates of divorce, teen pregnancy, and out-of-wedlock births than their Blue counterparts. But this isn't evidence of Red American hypocrisy, or stupidity; rather, it's evidence that lower-income Americans (Red states are generally poorer than Blue states) have been adversely affected by the dislocations and disarray that followed the Sexual Revolution, and have responded by embracing a conservative politics that promises to shore up the institutions that provide stability and support—their families, their churches, and their neighborhoods. As the *American Prospect*'s Garance Franke-Ruta has written:

> Lower-income individuals simply live in a much more disrupted society, with higher divorce rates, more single moms, more abortions, and more interpersonal and inter-family strife, than do the middle- and upper-middle class people they want to be like. It should come as no surprise that the politics of reaction is strongest where there is most to react to. People in states like Massachusetts, for example, which has very high per capita incomes and the lowest divorce rate in the country, are relatively unconcerned about gay marriage, while those in Southern states with much higher poverty, divorce, and single-parenthood rates feel the family to be threatened because family life is, in fact, much less stable in their communities.

The obvious liberal retort is that right-wing wedge issues like gay marriage are only tangentially related to the stability of heterosexual families, and that they are being used cynically by politicians who are unwilling to tackle the harder questions of what to do about illegitimacy and divorce. There's truth to this critique, but it's also slightly disingenuous: Whether gay marriage is a good idea or not, a great many of its supporters are the heirs of the liberal activists who insisted for decades that Moynihan's anxiety over black single parenthood represented a mix of "subtle racism" and contempt for the virtue of nontraditional "kinship networks"; who celebrated the decline of the two-parent family as a blessed liberation from the evils of patriarchy; and who mercilessly mocked Dan Quayle for daring to suggest that a wealthy single mother might not be the best role model for American women. For every gay-marriage advocate like Andrew Sullivan or Jonathan Rauch making the case for same-sex wedlock as an essentially conservative idea, there are a dozen intellectuals like the three hundred who signed the recent statement "Beyond Gay Marriage," arguing that gay unions ought to serve as a first step toward "legal recognition for a wide range of relationships, households and families—regardless of kinship or conjugal status." (In a follow-up to their landmark opinion on gay marriage, the judges of the Massachusetts Supreme Court remarked that if the legislative debate proved too difficult, it might make sense for the state to "jettison the term 'marriage' altogether.") Gay marriage may not be a major threat to heterosexual marriage in America, but it's likely to gain working-class support and spread beyond the bluest patches of America only insofar as it disentangles itself from this sort of liberationist agenda.

What the liberal critique of GOP-style social conservatism does identify, though, is the conservative habit of diagnosing the working class's cultural problems and then pretending that those problems are the only ones there are. In reality, you can't disentangle the sociological trends that have created familial instability from the economic trends, at home and worldwide, that have increased financial insecurity for working-class voters. Divorce and illegitimacy lead to economic disadvantage, but the reverse is also true, and understanding the working-class crisis requires starting with culture but then turning to economics as well.

Inequality and Insecurity

In considering the working class's economic difficulties, it's worth starting with what *isn't* true—namely, the oft-heard claim that working-class Americans have been pushed toward poverty over the last thirty years. This is a standard left-wing talking point that conceals a far more complicated picture.

Early in 2006, Stephen Rose, now a senior economic fellow with the center-left think tank Third Way, infuriated many to his left with a short paper called "The Trouble with Class-Interest Populism," in which he pointed out that as little as 23 percent of the American population "can be categorized as having a direct personal interest in supporting the social safety net programs that most of the public strongly associates with the Democratic party." For Rose, the economic story of recent decades is not one of immiseration but of gains for many working-class families. His most striking finding: When you average out family incomes over fifteen years and capture only the peak earning years—from ages 26 to 59—fully 60 percent of Americans will live in households making over $60,000 a year, with half of these households making over $85,000. This persistent prosperity, joined to the real economic gains that aren't picked up by income statistics—ranging from cheaper food and consumer products to better health care to larger homes to increased leisure time—has meant that most working-class Americans feel like beneficiaries of the changing economy rather than victims of it, even if their wages aren't rising the way they did during the long postwar boom.

As a result, they have felt comfortable voting for the GOP—or so it seemed until the 2006 election, which saw the rise of what Rahm Emanuel called "suburban populism." The Lou Dobbs Democrats, as we saw in the last chapter, appealed to workers in America's exurbs and office parks by picking up on two issues that are masked by Rose's averaging and by the general picture of working-class success. The first is inequality: Over the last thirty-five years, as we've seen, most of America's enormous economic gains have been concentrated in the hands of those with four-year college degrees—and over the past five years, in the hands of the top 1 percent, or indeed even the top 0.1 percent, of the income distribution. The second is insecurity: the fluctuations in annual income created by the globalized economy. This has made economic instability, not poverty or prosperity, a central concern of today's working class, whether you're talking about the small business owner who can barely afford health care or the autoworker who discovers that his corporate pension is a mirage.

Which is the greater problem? Many on the left would pick inequality, perceiving the growing gap between rich and poor not as a product of the free market and the long-widening gap between the college educated and the working class, but as the result of the use and abuse of political power. Traditionally, they note, American pay has kept pace with American productivity (the measure of how much workers produce per hour). When wages stagnated from the 1970s till the 1990s, productivity was stagnating, too. When they rebounded in the Clinton years, it was because productivity had rebounded as well. In the Bush years, though, something changed. Since 2001, real hourly pay for nonsupervisory workers has increased by a mere 3 percent, despite an 18 percent increase in economy-wide productivity. More striking still, economists Kenneth Scheve and Matthew Slaughter have observed that only workers with doctorates or professional graduate degrees, two categories that add up to just 3.4 percent of the total workforce, have seen an increase in mean real money earnings. To illustrate this stark divide, consider the case of Goldman Sachs, to some a powerful symbol of the new Gilded Age and to others a peerless corporate innovator. In 2006, the average hourly wage was just over $17. But for Goldman Sachs employees, the same average hourly wage was $200, and the firm's top traders made somewhere between $17,000 and $33,000 an hour.

A number of distinguished economists, *New York Times* columnist Paul Krugman most prominently among them, have argued that this explosion of what's called "upper-tail inequality" is less about individual productivity than it is about conservative ideology. For these new-model populists, the idea that inequality is the result of the widening income gap between the college educated and everyone else (and the fact that more and more compensation is taking the form of increasingly expensive health-care benefits rather than wages) is just an excuse for "denial and fatalism," as one of Krugman's most memorable columns put it. Instead, the real culprit behind rising inequality is a combination of corporate malfeasance and pro-rich economic activism, ranging from opposition to raising the minimum wage to a broader assault on the right to organize. This new-model populism's political tribune is Virginia senator Jim Webb, whose blistering response to President Bush's 2007 State of the Union took on the new bêtes noires of his compatriots on the left—America's CEOs. "When I graduated from college [in 1968]," he told the television audience, "the average corporate CEO made twenty times what the average worker did; today, it's nearly four hundred times. In other words, it takes the average worker more than a year to make the money that his or her boss makes in one day."

The obvious implication of these remarks is that there's something unfair and even crooked about soaring CEO pay, that this something has a great deal to do with GOP policies and thus can easily be undone by Democrats. In reality, though, the dramatic increase in CEO pay has largely been a natural outgrowth of a few mostly benign developments. Back when Webb graduated from college, CEO pay had been stagnant for years, in what is remembered as an era of corporate bloat. Only when private-equity firms came on the scene were the big multinationals shaken out of their torpor. In order to fight off these pinstripe pirates, corporate boards tried to gin up new ways to motivate executives.

Meanwhile, the death of corporate loyalty hit top executives as well as rank-and-file employees. More and more CEOs were hired from outside firms, and more and more CEOs were fired after a brief period of time. It makes sense that a talented executive would demand a generous severance package to soften the impact of getting sacked. Then, of course, there is the fact that the market capitalization of America's biggest corporations has exploded. If you're the sole person at the top of a major American company, a fixed slice of the pie will soon get very large. And if you're seen as indispensable to a company's market cap—imagine what would happen to Apple if Steve Jobs decided to leave Cupertino to become a Buddhist monk—you're "worth" a heck of a lot. (Indeed, Paul Krugman's own success is a perfect example of this phenomenon: He's a beneficiary of what the economist Sherwin Rosen called the "superstar" syndrome, in which a few celebrities in each field, from Michael Jordan to CEOs such as Jobs, reap enormous rewards for their talents.)

Had CEO pay remained at what you might call the Webb ratio, it's almost certain that today's top executives would find more lucrative opportunities elsewhere in the business world. The same logic applies to others in the upper strata of the new inequality. Hedge funds, which have spawned dozens of billionaires in recent years, have helped accelerate economic growth by making capital markets more efficient. The billionaires in question are thus capturing only a small part of the wealth they've created.

More broadly, if we can finger an institutional culprit behind rising inequality, one of the strongest candidates might be the rise in "performance pay," when workers are explicitly rewarded on the basis of productivity. (That accounts, at least in part, for the disparity *within* the ranks of Goldman Sachs employees.) Of course it's easy to see how such incentives might contribute to overall productivity growth without spreading the gains from that growth around equally. A ban on performance pay or an end to it might bring us closer to the postwar norm of economic solidarity in the workplace, but it's not clear that it would make workers, including poor workers, better off.

There's also America's changing demographic composition to consider. The American population is older and more educated now than it's ever been, and older and more educated populations tend to be more unequal. The members of a young and uneducated population tend to have relatively few options, which means you're unlikely to see too many highfliers emerge from their ranks. The old and educated, in contrast, have had years to diverge: Some develop good habits or at least good luck, others encounter serious misfortune that is compounded over time, and still others decide to drop out of the rat race by moving to low-cost and low-wage parts of the country or by simply choosing to live with less.

What happens when we control for America's demographic composition and assess the factors driving inequality? According to Thomas Lemieux of the University of British Columbia, doing so would account for much of the observed increase in residual income inequality. And of course the bulk of income inequality can be attributed to, you guessed it, experience and education, the standard human capital variables Krugman and the rest of the new-model populists treat as secondary.

This isn't to say there's nothing wrong with spiraling inequality. It's just that there is no conspiracy behind it. Instead, we're left with the traditional story: a big and growing gap between those with college degrees and those without them, and a gap between those with college degrees and those with postgraduate degrees that is bigger and growing even faster. Both are troubling, but neither are amenable to easy policy fixes. To be sure, simply asserting that "more people should go to college" is an inadequate response to American workers facing a future of slow wage growth or worse. (Scheve and Slaughter, in a sobering back-of-the-envelope calculation, estimate that it would take forty years before the United States could increase the college-graduate share of the workforce to 50 percent from 33 percent.) Yet railing against CEO bonuses and "windfall profits," cathartic though it may be, fails to get at what's really ailing American workers, and it may actually prove counterproductive. Krugman and company are right to suggest that there is much more we can do to mitigate inequality. But there's a real risk that their diagnosis will lead us toward the wrong solutions.

Which is why a number of liberal voices, like Jacob Hacker, author of *The Great Risk Shift,* are focusing on working-class *anxiety*—over health care, pensions, and income volatility—rather than inequality. Economic instability, Hacker argues, has risen faster than inequality over the last thirty years. In 1970, the typical American family had a 7 percent chance of experiencing a 50 percent drop in their income in a given year; since then, according his calculations, the risk of such a drop has more than doubled, to 16 percent. The number of households filing for bankruptcy multiplied sevenfold between 1980 and 2005; the mortgage foreclosure rate has multiplied fivefold. Meanwhile, health-care costs are rising and employer-provided plans are cutting back on benefits, and the same is happening with pensions. All of these risk shifts disproportionately impact the working class, who are more likely to be plunged into poverty by a sudden income swing and less likely to have reserves of capital to fall back on.

Hacker's estimates paint a bleak picture of the American economy, and his work stirred up considerable controversy among policy wonks. Some have pointed out that he gives short shrift to the fact that even as income has grown more volatile, many working-class families have adapted successfully, smoothing their consumption through the use of debt and then servicing the debt rather than letting it drag them down into poverty. Others have suggested that Hacker underestimates the extent to which income volatility is actually a critical component of America's economic resilience in the face of growing global competition. (With raises stuck below inflation for most workers, job-hopping is increasingly the best way to get ahead; indeed, one problem with today's economy may be that workers aren't engaging in *enough* job-hopping.) Meanwhile, a number of recent studies suggest that Hacker's most alarming findings are, well, wrong, and that individual earnings volatility has actually remained fairly steady over the past two decades.

Still, part of Hacker's argument rings true; it just isn't the part he chooses to emphasize. In his chapter on divorce, which could have been the heart of *The Great Risk Shift,* Hacker breezes over the link between family breakdown and increasing economic insecurity—perhaps because the phenomenon suggests a cultural solution as much as an economic one and doesn't lend itself to an easy demonization of the political Right. But the family is the area of society where his thesis seems correct. Individual income volatility may not have changed much since the 1970s, but *family* income volatility has risen by at least 24 percent. This means that working-class families are caught on the horns of a dilemma: Wage pressures make two incomes a necessity for more and more couples, but children are more likely to become discipline problems when both parents work long hours, and the stress caused by a heavy workload has also been found to exacerbate the rate of divorce, which cripples families and stymies economic advancement. As a result, working-class parents have to work longer and harder to give their children a decent chance, but working longer and harder might actually imperil the well-being of their children and their marriages.

The result is anxiety amid affluence, economic stress amid stock-market highs. As Republican pollster David Winston found in a survey conducted in early 2007, working-class voters resent the idea that they simply don't appreciate how great the economy *really* is, with low inflation, low unemployment, and relatively high growth. That's the message that too many conservatives have been pushing, and it's done considerable harm to the Republican brand. Though the new economy and the new sexual order both offer more freedom and independence, they also vastly multiply the bad decisions a family can make. Even when this insecurity doesn't send working-class voters slipping downward, it definitely makes it harder for them to leap forward. Rising inequality and increasing risk aren't immiserating Sam's Club voters, but they're making it tougher to ever leave the working class behind.

Norberto Felix-Cruz, a Mexican American high-school student, put it best to journalist Katherine Boo in the pages of *The New Yorker*:

> "People say, 'Oh, your family can't get ahead,' but actually we get ahead all the time," he said. "It's just that then one of the trucks breaks—my dad and I need them for the jobs—or one of my parents is out of work, then we slip right back down."

Young men like Norberto, enterprising, family-minded, and intelligent, represent a promising American future. Yet for too many of them, the effort to make it into a stable middle-class life feels Sisyphean, and the result is a rising sympathy for the political Left, with its promise of equality-through-redistribution. A recent Pew survey of American public opinion since 1987, for instance, found that the percentage of Americans who agree that "it is the responsibility of the government to take care of people who can't take care of themselves" has risen steadily since 1994, from 57 percent to 69 percent. So has the percentage agreeing that the government should "help more needy people even if debt increases," which has climbed from 41 percent to 54 percent. (In both cases, this shift has occurred among Republican voters as well as Democrats.) The percentage subscribing to the statement "today it's really true that the rich just get richer while the poor get poorer" reached 73 percent in 2007, the highest level recorded since the early-1990s recession, and nearly all of the increase came among middle-income voters; meanwhile, the percentage of Americans describing themselves as "working class," rather than "middle class," has risen sharply as well.

Young people in particular—the Norbertos of the world—are more favorable to government interventions than their elders. Just as the overregulated, overtaxed economic climate of the 1970s made Generation X the most Republican generation in recent history, the current climate of anxiety and inequality is having precisely the opposite effect and pushing Generation Y into the arms of the Democrats.

Indeed, on domestic policy, the Republican Party isn't just out of touch with the country as a whole; it's increasingly out of touch with its own base. In May of 2005, the Pew Research Center released its Political Typology, a survey that slices the American electorate into nine discrete groups. Unsurprisingly, the core of the GOP's support turns out to be drawn from "Enterprisers," affluent, optimistic, and staunchly conservative on economic and social issues alike. But the so-called Enterprisers represent just 11 percent of registered voters, and apart from them, the most reliable GOP voters are Social Conservatives (13 percent of registered voters) and Pro-Government Conservatives (10 percent of voters). Both groups are predominantly female (Enterprisers are overwhelmingly male); both are critical of big business; and both, significantly, support more government involvement—even at the cost of higher taxes—to alleviate the economic risks faced by a growing number of families.

As we've seen, this turn toward the welfare state is less a response to growing poverty than to rising insecurity and inequality—and more important, to rising fears of socioeconomic stratification, which is the greatest domestic danger facing American society and the real source of conservatives' growing political peril. Inequality and instability only undermine a democratic order when the lower classes feel like there aren't enough ladders leading upward. We don't envy the rich if we think that our kids have a chance of joining them, and we're more likely to accept significant risk if the chances for significant rewards are great as well. This promise of mobility and opportunity has long been the conservative movement's trump card: So long as Americans believe that the poor can rise by their own efforts (and the rich can fall), they're likely to resist efforts to create a European-style nanny state that curtails independence in the name of universal security.

But such mobility is increasingly at risk, as two of the major post-sixties trends in American society—increased meritocracy at the top of society and immigration at the bottom—threaten to freeze the social order in amber.

The Trouble with Meritocracy

Consider college admissions—one of the defining moments of every young American's life, if you believe the press it gets. For a parent drowning in glossy brochures, an admissions dean deluged with applications, or a student padding a résumé with A.P.

exams and extracurriculars, it's easy to see applying to college as a universal American rite of passage, ushering each successive generation of stressed-out applicants into the anteroom of adulthood.

But for most American teenagers, the admissions process is something else entirely—a game that's rigged against them, if they play at all. The overall figures are stark: If you hope to obtain a bachelor's degree from an American college by age twenty-four, your chances are roughly fifty-fifty if you come from a family with an income over $90,000 a year; one-in-four if your family income falls between $61,000 and $91,000; and slightly better than one-in-ten between $35,000 and $61,000. And for high schoolers whose parents make less than $35,000 a year—which is to say, a quarter of all American teens—the chances of earning a degree by age twenty-four are just slightly over one in twenty.

It would be an exaggeration to say that where and whether you'll go to college is entirely a matter of birth, breeding, and income bracket; native intelligence and academic merit still lift the boats of numerous poor students. But at the very least, academic achievement is so bound up with social class that separating the two is practically impossible. Even when you attempt to do so—culling out the "deserving" poor from the undeserving, based on grades or SAT scores—wealthier students are still much more likely to attend college than their high-scoring counterparts in the working class.

This wasn't how the modern meritocracy was supposed to work. American higher education was overhauled in the middle years of the twentieth century to be a force for near-universal opportunity, or so the overhaulers imagined. Widespread use of the SAT would find working-class kids with low grades but high "scholastic aptitude," as the acronym then had it, and elevate them to the academic level they deserved, while need-based financial aid and government grants would ensure that everyone who wanted a college education could afford to pay. But today, college-going may actually be *more* stratified than it was in 1970. More Americans go to college than ever before, but most of the gains in degree attainment, particularly at selective four-year colleges, have been made by students from the upper and upper-middle classes. Whereas through boom and recession, war and peace, the percentage of Americans from the poorest quarter of the population who obtain college degrees by age twenty-four has remained constant, hovering around 6 percent.

This stratification has something to do with the self-interest of universities, which have a strong financial incentive to admit wealthy students and turn away working-class applicants who often can't pay the full freight. It has something to do with the power of Bobo voters, the class that wields the most influence over the politics of higher education, who have pushed for a variety of changes to financial aid policy—moving from grants to loans, say, or shifting from need-based to merit-based financial aid—that tend to reinforce their own advantages. But it's too simple to blame the lack of socioeconomic diversity in higher education on the self-interest of universities or the pandering of politicians. There's also the uncomfortable fact that a society in which education is unevenly distributed may represent less a failure of meritocracy than its logical endpoint.

This was the fear of Michael Young, the British civil servant who coined the term "meritocracy" in the 1950s and whose novel *The Rise of the Meritocracy*—written in the form of a dry Ph.D. thesis analyzing society from the vantage point of 2034—envisioned a future of ever-more-perfect intelligence tests and educational segregation, in which a cognitive elite holds sway over the less-intelligent masses until the stupid rise to overthrow their brainy masters. Such a scenario of stratification-by-intelligence was raised again in the early 1990s by Richard Herrnstein and Charles Murray, in their ripe-for-controversy best-seller *The Bell Curve*. The book is now best remembered for suggesting the existence of ineradicable racial differences in IQ, but its larger argument was that America is increasingly stratified "according to cognitive ability." Meritocracy, they argue, co-opts the brightest working-class Americans and incorporates them into the upper class, leaving the less-favored masses stuck below. By segregating the intelligent and ensuring that they'll socialize only with one another, America risks re-creating the class structure of the Old World, based on brainpower instead of blood.

From the present vantage point, both Young's dystopian fears and *The Bell Curve*'s self-consciously hardheaded realism seem too simplistic, since both reduce the complex question of merit and success to a matter of IQ-based intelligence, easily tested and easily graphed. The picture is more complicated than this, and the exact role that inherited intelligence plays in personal success remains muddy and controversial, with most scholars rejecting the "Herrnstein nightmare" (as Mickey Kaus dubbed it) of stratification-by-IQ.

But for the purposes of understanding the contemporary American scene, it doesn't really matter whether our meritocracy passes on success genetically, given how thoroughly it's passed on through class and culture. It's not just that wealthier students are likely to attend better schools, or have more stable families and fewer behavioral problems, or score higher on the SATs (which were intended to be class-neutral aptitude tests, but turned out to be amenable to gaming by expensive tutors and study guides). It's that the higher you go up the income ladder, the greater the emphasis on education, from infancy to adolescence; the greater the pressure, from parents and peers, to excel—and the greater the likelihood that you will. Nor does it matter if you change the criteria for "success" to involvement in extracurriculars, say, or community service—the advantage will still go to the kids who are taught to value those activities. (Even the admissions boost many schools give to recruited athletes, which is often assumed to help low-income students, actually tends to disproportionately benefit the children of upper-income families.)

In this inherited meritocracy, success reinforces success: The high-achieving kid will not only attend school with other high-achievers, he'll marry a high-achiever and then move with her to a high-achieving area—the better to ensure that his child will have all the same cultural advantages that he enjoyed growing up. Thus the country's mass upper class becomes increasingly geographically segregated from the rest of the population, insulating themselves from the wider culture and killing off the local civic institutions that they used to sustain. It's a phenomenon that's been proceeding apace for the past thirty years. According to Richard Florida, who coined the term "creative class" to describe the new elite, human capital—that is, college-educated Americans—is increasingly concentrated in a small group of American cities, the San Joses and Denvers and Bostons, while the rest of the country remains disproportionately working class. As he points out, roughly half the residents in cities like San Francisco and Washington, D.C., boast four-year college degrees, compared to just 11 percent in Cleveland and 14 percent in Detroit. The gulf in postgraduate degrees is just as striking: A fifth of Seattle's residents have an advanced degree, compared to just 2 percent of the inhabitants of Newark.

"Creative class" cities, not coincidentally, are increasingly hostile environments for people who don't arrive at their gates with deep pockets and advanced degrees. Their huge pools of wealth, their sky-high real estate prices, and their strict zoning regulations, Joel Kotkin points out, has transformed their professional class "into a kind of landed gentry," borne ever upward by their income from rents, dividends, and interest. These are great places to be a baby boomer who bought a home twenty years ago, and good places to be one of their yuppie children; they're places whose housing booms are built on countless town houses and apartments and recreation centers for moneyed singles and cohabiting couples, and where the deck is stacked in favor of the extended adolescence characteristic of the mass upper class. And they're places where young Americans of modest means who choose to marry, start a family, and begin sacrificing for the next generation find themselves forced into crowded apartments and long commutes, which adds another set of stresses to familial instability and economic insecurity.

Small wonder that these "Euro-American" cities, as Kotkin calls them, are increasingly distinguished by the absence of children: Seattle, perhaps the prototypical "creative class" city, has about as many residents as it did in 1960, but only half the number of children. San Francisco, rather more impressively, has more dogs than children (some of these pets no doubt live in greater comfort than many of their human neighbors). In places where zoning rules prohibit backyards and municipal governments subsidize loft apartments, where public schools are mediocre and private schools expensive, and owning a home requires $150,000 a year, children are closer to a luxury good than an investment in the future. Small wonder, too, that middle-income voters are abandoning cities: New York, for instance, is increasingly divided between neighborhoods where everyone is part of the mass upper class and neighborhoods inhabited by the working poor, a pattern that a recent Brookings Institution study found in high-density areas around the country. What remains of the working class is largely employed by these cities' burgeoning public sectors, hauling trash and running trains for the well-off and well educated.

So Sam's Club voters either stay and struggle, or they move out—to the suburbs and exurbs, or the new "aspirational cities" of the American West, the Boises and Renos and Oklahoma Cities. They may thrive there, but the result is still a nation whose social classes are less likely to mix than ever before and whose heights are out of reach for those not born to them—which leads in turn to a sense of polarization that's geographic, socio-economic, and cultural all at once. The ultimate effect was described aptly by Christopher Lasch as a trend "in the direction of a two-class society in which the favored few monopolize the advantages of money, education and power."

The Trouble with Immigration

Worse, as meritocracy pulls the mass upper class upward, mass immigration threatens to pull the working class downward. Large-scale immigration from Mexico has been good for the economy as a whole, but like so many recent economic trends, it has made the rich richer and the poor more insecure. The college educated have reaped the benefits of a steep decrease in the price of labor-intensive services, while low-skilled Americans, exposed to increasingly stiff competition, have seen their earnings stagnate and even dwindle. African Americans, in particular, have suffered as immigration has risen: A recent study suggests that immigration accounts for roughly a third of the overall decline in the black employment rate over the last forty years.

But immigrants aren't just the cause of growing inequality—they're inequality's victims as well. Immigration advocates insist that the current influx of Mexicans will assimilate the way earlier generations did, and up to a point they're right. Despite conservative fears, immigrants from Mexico are making impressive progress in education, English acquisition, and intermarriage, matching or exceeding the gains made by earlier generations and by newcomers from other nations today. The trouble is that *economic* assimilation rates are dramatically affected by overall economic inequality, a factor beyond the control of even the most hardworking immigrant, and today's economic climate is far less favorable to assimilation than the America of the early twentieth century.

Immigrants from Southern and Eastern Europe who arrived

in the early 1900s benefited from what seemed to be an ever-expanding middle class. Fifty years later, Mexican immigrants have had the opposite experience, entering the American workforce at a moment when middle-income wages are harder and harder for workers without a college degree to attain. As Joel Perlmann points out in *Italians Then, Mexicans Now*, his study of assimilation patterns, an Italian or Pole who arrived in the United States in 1910 at twenty-five earned roughly 65 percent of the prevailing white wage; by the time he reached retirement age, his wages were up to 70 percent of the prevailing rate. By contrast, a Mexican American who arrived in the United States at twenty-five in 1970 could expect to earn 70 percent of the prevailing white wage; by the time he reached age fifty-five, in 2000, he was earning only 47 percent—even though his education levels and English fluency would have likely increased over that time. This gap narrows but persists in the second generation: Today's second-generation Mexican Americans can expect to earn 73 percent of the prevailing white wage; by contrast, second-generation immigrants in the first half of the century could expect to earn between 84 percent and 96 percent of the prevailing wage.

Optimists point out that when you control for education, the Mexican-white wage gap disappears. But this is actually the crux of the problem. You need *many* more years of education to be competitive in the American economy today than you did in, say, the 1930s, and so "controlling" for education is like waving a statistical wand over the problem and hoping it disappears. Whereas fewer than 9 percent of native-born men are high-school dropouts, 63 percent of Mexican-born workers in the United States have never finished high school. The gap closes in subsequent generations, but it closes *slowly*: In 2000, for instance, 30 percent of second-generation Mexican Americans aged twenty-five to thirty-four lacked a high-school diploma, compared to just 9 percent of whites; in the race to get a college education, just 8 percent of second-generation Mexican Americans obtained bachelor's degrees, compared to 30 percent of whites. Meanwhile, a recent report by the Educational Testing Service suggests that by 2030, mass immigration may push America's literacy rate into decline for the first time in a hundred years.

This is bad news for immigrants and the native-born working class alike, who share the costs of slowed assimilation. The debate over immigration usually revolves around its impact on economic growth and on working-class wages. But there's also the strain on the welfare system. The child poverty rate for Hispanics is up 43 percent since 1990; in the same period, the numbers of black and white children in poverty declined 16.9 percent and 18.5 percent, respectively. Hispanics account for 60 percent of the increase of Americans without health insurance since 1990, and single parenthood among Hispanics rose from 25 percent in 1980 to 34 percent in 2000. These kinds of numbers inevitably impose higher costs on government and working-class taxpayers. In 2001, 34 percent of households headed by Mexican immigrants used one of the major welfare programs (unemployment compensation, subsidized school lunches, food stamps, Temporary Assistance for Needy Families [TANF], and so forth), compared to 15 percent of native households; 29 percent relied on Medicaid for health-care costs, compared to 12 percent of households headed by native-born Americans. Although overall poverty rates decline in the second Mexican American generation, the use of welfare programs remains nearly as high as in the first.

The frustrations and failures associated with the slow path to assimilation also may explain a crime-rate paradox—namely, the fact that first-generation immigrants commit crimes at lower rates than the white population, while their (theoretically better-off) children and grandchildren commit crimes at higher rates. Some sociologists have argued that immigrants are simply assimilating to the high-crime norms of the United States, but this is specious: Second-generation Hispanic immigrants don't replicate native-born rates of violence, they exceed them dramatically. So among men eighteen to thirty-nine, less than 1 percent of foreign-born Mexicans are incarcerated—but 6 percent of native-born Americans of Mexican descent are in prison, three times the rate for native-born non-Hispanic whites. Overall, Hispanics represented 13 percent of the U.S. population in 2000, but accounted for 31 percent of inmates in the federal criminal justice system.

What's happening isn't that second-generation immigrants are assimilating to American norms; rather, a portion of the immigrant population, frustrated with stagnating wages and an economy that's less favorable to high-school graduates than fifty years ago, ends up dropping out of the system and assimilating downward, toward the behaviors associated with the poorest native-born whites and blacks. Economists call this "segmentation"—a process in which one group of immigrants moves up the ladder of success while another group falls off, assimilating not upward into the culture of the middle class but down into the habits and mores of the underclass. As this cohort increases in size—and if immigration continues at the present level, it's hard to see how it won't—the natural tendency will be for inequality to increase, creating ever more distance, cultural as well as economic, between the top of American society and the increasingly Hispanic working class.

The Nightmare Scenario

The good news is many of these trends are still in their (relative) infancy: Most Americans still marry and most children are still born into two-parent families; the working class is insecure but still reasonably prosperous; social mobility is stagnating or declining slightly, but not precipitously; America is not nearly as culturally polarized as the culture-war shouting matches would suggest. The mediating institutions of our culture—families, churches, community organizations—are weaker than they used to be, but they're still resilient. The laid-off factory worker can retrain himself with a distance-education degree and land on his feet. The economically stressed family can leave Boston for Phoenix or Sioux City and find new friends in a megachurch or a sprinkler-fed subdivision. And all of them are cushioned by America's constantly expanding economy and our immense capacity for wealth-generation.

But the amount of stress on working-class Americans keeps going up, and at some point the Sam's Club demographic is going to stop treading water and start sinking. Whatever happens will probably happen slowly: America isn't going to turn into Argentina overnight. But we might start to look more and more like Great Britain, where the working class is exposed to the same pressures as their cousins in the United States, but with darker consequences. The process of family breakdown, in particular, is far more advanced in Great Britain than it is here: The illegitimacy rate is 41 percent in England and Wales, and it's 46 percent among native-born women; England's heavily Asian foreign-born population actually brings the rate of out-of-wedlock births *down*. This epidemic of fatherlessness goes a long way toward explaining why the crime rate in Britain resembles the dark days of crack-epidemic America: There are more murders in today's United States, largely because we have more guns, but the crime rate as a whole is some 40 percent higher in the United Kingdom—more burglaries and carjackings, more thefts and more assaults. And it explains, as well, the seemingly irreversible coarsening of working-class life in Britain—the public drunkenness, the soccer hooliganism, the pop-culture vulgarism that makes America look puritanical, the epidemic of rowdiness that led the Labour government to attempt a crackdown on "nuisance" behavior, and the kind of cultural pessimism that defined the United States in the 1970s.

This is the most likely scenario for a near-future America—no cultural Armageddons or dramatic collapses; just a slow but steady degradation of everyday working-class life under the pressures of rising illegitimacy, insecurity, and stratification. This, in turn, will make economic populism ever more politically potent, for the reasons suggested by economists Alberto Alesina and George-Marios Angeletos:

If a society believes that individual effort determines income, and that all have a right to enjoy the fruits of their effort, it will choose low redistribution and low taxes. In equilibrium, effort will be high, the role of luck limited, market outcomes will be quite fair, and social beliefs will be self-fulfilled. If instead a society believes that luck, birth, connections and/or corruption determine wealth, it will tax a lot, thus distorting allocations and making these beliefs self-sustained as well.

But even this picture may be too optimistic, because there are trends developing outside America's borders that put more than just the working class's prospects at risk. We're entering the age of the Global Labor Glut. In this—and only this—regard, the most alarmist critics of free trade could be right.

In hindsight, the most important historical event of the 1990s may have been economic rather than political—not the collapse of the Soviet Union, but what Harvard economist Richard Freeman calls the "Great Doubling." Within a remarkably short period of time, a decade at most, workers in Eastern Europe, the former Soviet Union, India, and China flooded into the global labor market. Because these countries had isolated themselves from the American-led global economy on political grounds, and because they had fairly large internal markets, they were in a sense economic nonentities as far as the prosperous global economy built around New York, London, and Tokyo was concerned. Surrounded by trade barriers, drawing on self-contained capital markets, exporting only small numbers of migrants, these countries' elites controlled economic life rigidly. Some kind of economic opening had to happen sooner or later, but when it came it happened all at once. Had the Soviet bloc, China, and India remained *outside* the global economy, the global labor market would have a pool of around 1.46 billion workers. Instead, the sudden opening of these economies gave us *2.93* billion workers as of 2000—hence the "Great Doubling."

But while labor doubled, capital did not. For a time, at least, the Great Doubling conformed to the basic understanding of North-South trade, in which the developed world sheds less-skilled, low-wage jobs to the developing world but gains skilled high-wage jobs in return. This was bad news for the American working class, as we've seen, but the mass upper class continued to prosper. As it turns out, though, China and India were pouring resources into higher education, creating a vast pool of *skilled* labor even more impressive than their larger pool of less-skilled labor. These workers can do more than assemble televisions or automobiles: They can take part in cutting-edge research, providing sophisticated financial services and even advanced medical care—all at a fraction of the cost of American workers. The proportion of educated workers in China and India is still minuscule. But their absolute number is extraordinary, and more than enough to increase wage pressure on even the best-educated American workers. Durable goods, it turns out, aren't the only things you can trade. Knowledge can also be exported, and even the most highly educated workers in the developed world are facing increasingly stiff competition.

Which will mean, in turn, that the mass upper class may find itself subjected to the same economic trends that have buffeted working-class Americans over the last thirty years. Indeed, they're already feeling some pain: Over the last five years, during an extraordinary economic boom, average compensation for college graduates had barely kept pace with inflation. When you factor out the most successful college graduates, the CEOs and superstar economists and Goldman Sachs employees, the picture is one of outright wage stagnation. And a closer look at the numbers shows that it's young adults who've been hit the hardest. For college graduates between twenty-five and thirty-four, the women and men who are trying to gain an economic foothold and start families of their own, real earnings fell by 8 percent between 2002 and 2006.

If we're right about the likely effects of the global labor glut, this decline isn't just a blip on the radar screen. It's likely to be followed by real economic pain. Guild rules will protect some of the most privileged professionals, but the ranks of middle management will be thinned as routine information processing is automated at a breakneck pace. This trend may not stop until it gets uncomfortably close to the boardroom. Instead of a country where a third of the population, the mass upper class, gains ground while the working class runs in place—our current predicament—we could be moving toward a landscape in which the vast majority of the country finds itself losing ground and only the very richest Americans continue to thrive. This will be good news for exactly one sector of the American economy: luxury personal services. Assuming that the capital rich are still thriving in the America of the future, they will be able to spend quite a lot of money on servants. The nightmare of a servile working class, resisted by Lincoln and the New Dealers, will finally become a reality.

If this scenario comes to pass, the Thomas Franks of the world will get their wish and economics will trump every other political issue. This could betoken the rise of a more Latin American politics, rife with populism and xenophobia; more likely, though, it will simply make America look more and more like Europe. Living under conditions of diminished earnings power and worsening job security, it's easy to imagine even well-off Americans growing resentful of the ultra-rich and calling for far more redistribution and a vastly expanded welfare state. This is to say nothing of the working-class population, where family dissolution has already hobbled the ability of millions to save and build wealth. For those living paycheck to paycheck, the prospect of government interference seems far less frightening than the prospect of government indifference, particularly when you've been trained to never accept responsibility for your own actions and your own failures.

What would a Europeanized United States look like? Imagine higher taxes, vastly expanded public-sector employment, infantilized upper-middle-class men and women who live with their parents until their late thirties because their jobs don't pay them enough to buy a house of their own, illegitimacy rising toward 50 percent and a growing social services bureaucracy that steps in to pick up the slack, plunging birthrates as rearing children grows ever more expensive, and an ever-larger stream of immigrants being imported to fill the breach. For many of America's elites, this scenario might not sound so uncongenial. But a victory for this vision of the American future would be a defeat for everything that has been distinctive about American life.

Instead, we need a political program that recognizes the danger that we face and does everything possible to resist it. In the next three chapters, we attempt to sketch the outlines of what such a politics might look like. Our proposals are neither perfect nor exhaustive, but they offer a starting place for a discussion about the working class's future, and the country's, that America needs to have.

7

Putting Families First

Any agenda for a working-class majority needs to begin at home, with an attempt to reverse the destructive cycle of the past thirty years, in which illegitimacy and familial instability breed financial anxiety among working-class families, which leads to further strains on family life, and so on. Crafting policies that stand against this trend is not a question of turning back the clock to some lost Ozzie-and-Harriet golden age, as critics of social conservatism often assert. Quite the opposite: Precisely because the world has changed, with the demise of lifetime employment and increasing returns to education, strong families are growing ever more important, and policies that encourage people to form them and keep them together are ever more necessary.

Such policies would doubtless meet with resistance from the childless and the privileged. But government support for economically insecure families wouldn't be money for nothing. America, like any nation, depends on parents' willingness to raise healthy and well-educated children. Without a youthful population, the costs of supporting retirees are unsustainable, and the innovation and entrepreneurial zeal that make America the world's economic leader will slowly wither. Childless people are free riders, in a sense, on the investment made by parents. Yet the decision to raise children continues to be treated as something akin to the decision to buy an expensive automobile—a perfectly fine thing to do, but don't expect any sympathy or support when you can't afford a tune-up or an oil change. Having a large family used to be a sign that you had faith in the future. Today, outside the family-friendly exurbs that played a crucial role in past Republican success, it's become a form of conspicuous consumption—or, for the poor, a mark of irresponsibility. This needs to change.

Putting Parents First

A family-friendly tax reform—a reform that keeps taxes lowest for young families making investments in their offspring—is an obvious place to start. The most promising proposal on this front belongs to *National Review*'s Ramesh Ponnuru, who has proposed a comprehensive, revenue-neutral reform that simplifies the tax code dramatically, reduces taxes on investment while doing away with the majority of itemized deductions, and massively expands the tax credit for children—from the current $1,000 to $5,000 per child. This credit would be indexed to wages and grow over time, and it would be available to all parents up to the amount that they pay in income *and* payroll taxes. Essentially, the plan would treat children as a species of investment, one that is currently overtaxed.

Some conservatives are likely to object that making the tax code more family friendly would eliminate too many people from the tax rolls every year, thus increasing the public's appetite for government spending by making it seem like a free lunch. But if anything, the opposite might be the case. Parents would be removed from the rolls only temporarily: As Ponnuru puts it, such a reform "would take low-income and middle-income people off the tax rolls while they raise children, and put them back on when they are through." And by delivering financial relief during the portion of the life cycle when Americans face the highest economic stresses, a family-friendly tax reform seems likely to make parents *less* likely to look to the welfare state for support.

Others, both liberals and conservatives, will assert that the childless already bear part of the cost of childrearing, in the form of the taxes that go to fund public schools. But these costs are a wash, not a sacrifice. As Cesar Conda and Robert Stein have noted, making the case for a similar "tax cuts for kids" approach to reform in the *Weekly Standard*, "When nonparents complain about having to pay school-related taxes, they are saying, in effect, that they were entitled to a free K-12 education without ever having to pay for one."

In an ideal world, such a tax reform ought to be specifically *marriage* friendly, targeted to married couples (and extended to widows and widowers, and possibly divorcées) and withheld from single and cohabiting parents. In post-sixties America, of course, this seems hopelessly draconian. Ponnuru, making the case for his tax plan, argues that it's politically unrealistic to advocate policies that "discriminate among children based on their parents' marital status." For now, he's probably right, which is why his tax plan is the best short-term approach for a Sam's Club conservatism to take. But given how many problems—from crime and drugs to inequality and economic insecurity—orbit around the rising rate of out-of-wedlock births, America needs to reckon seriously with the damage done by illegitimacy, and the importance of policies that privilege married couples, and reward them for doing right by their children. Politicians talk piously about the importance of the family, of course, and both sides in the gay marriage debate cast themselves as "strengthening" marriage. But if we're really serious about making the institution stronger, rather than accepting its slow-motion eclipse, then we should to be willing to stigmatize illegitimacy indirectly by tying tax relief to responsible parenting.

Giving a direct financial boost to families with children is one avenue of reform a Sam's Club agenda might explore; doing more to indirectly ease the burdens of working mothers (and fathers) is another. Balancing motherhood with employment is perhaps the hardest challenge facing American women in the postfeminist era, at least if you believe the dispatches from the "mommy wars" that climb best-seller lists every year. It's not a challenge for everyone: As the sociologist Neil Gilbert has pointed out, a substantial minority of American women are either "postmodern" (childless and devoted entirely to their careers) or "traditional" (content to stay home with the kids full-time and financially capable of doing so). But the majority of women are somewhere in the middle, attempting to balance their interest in paid work with their desire to be heavily involved in raising their families. "Women with one child normally tip the scales in favor of their careers," Gilbert writes, "while the group with two children leans more toward domestic life." But neither group is satisfied with the balance, and they are ill served by contemporary family policy.

To address the concerns of women with young children, liberals tend to focus on universal day care, parental leave, and other measures that are better understood as "business friendly" than as "family friendly," in that the goal is to make it as easy as possible for parents to maximize their time in the paid labor force. There's a good reason for this. Women's educational attainment has risen rapidly, surpassing that of younger men, and workplace success has followed. There is no returning to an economy, or a society, in which most women don't work outside of the home.

But not every working woman always wants to work full-time, particularly when her children are young, and those who recoil from the idea of day care should have other options—particularly since there's a great deal of data to suggest that very young children are poorly served by day care programs. Moreover, the feminist idealization of workplace success is to a certain extent an artifact of upper-middle-class privilege: If you're an assistant manager at Wal-Mart or a clerical worker in an office park, you're more likely to think of your work as a necessary but onerous way to make a living than a badge of empowerment. As family life has become increasingly economically insecure, forcing parents to work longer hours to keep up, more and more working women seem to feel the strain. A recent Pew survey found that only one in five working mothers with children under seventeen stated that full-time work is the "ideal situation" for them, compared to 32 percent in 1997. The rest either preferred part-time work (60 percent, up from 48 percent a decade ago) or not working at all outside the home (19 percent). And similar trends are at work among stay-at-home moms. The same survey found that only 16 percent would rather be working full-time outside the home, down from 24 percent in 1997, and nearly half stated that doing no work outside the home at all would be their ideal, up 9 percentage points in a decade.

These women form a natural constituency for a conservative politics that aims for greater flexibility in the workplace. Such a politics would recognize that many mothers are ill served by the modern American career track, which was designed to accommodate single-breadwinner men, and to that end assumes a seamless transition from school to full-time employment, with a career path that begins in the early twenties and continues in unbroken ascent until retirement. For many women, this is an appealing model, but many others—particularly in the working class—find themselves unable to contemplate taking time off while they bear and raise their children, because to do so would be to sabotage their careers and court unacceptable financial risk.

For these women (and for many men, as well), a better way

to approach the division between work and family life might be what Gilbert calls a "life-course perspective," with measures that would allow either parent to provide child care full-time for several years before entering, or reentering, the workforce. For instance, the government could offer subsidies to parents who provide child care in the home and pension credits that reflect the economic value of years spent in household labor. Or again, it could offer tuition credits for years spent rearing children, which could be exchanged for postgraduate or vocational education. These would be modeled on veterans' benefits—and that would be entirely appropriate, since both military service and parenthood are crucial to the country's well-being.

The Case for Sprawl

But the cost of raising children isn't just counted in babysitters hired and salary dollars forgone—as we saw in the previous chapter, it's counted in the rising price of real estate in the crowded cities and inner-ring suburbs of the East and West coasts. Which is why a Sam's Club agenda needs to be attuned to the interests of people trying to move further out to find living space—to the growing exurbs, the land of office parks and megachurches and voters with "some college," those upwardly mobile working-class Americans who have fled the congested cities to give their children room to breathe.

If you believe forty years of Hollywood stereotypes, of course, these suburban landscapes are defined by anomie and alienation. But recent research suggests that the suburbs and the exurbs actually *increase* the kind of civic participation and social networking that are crucial to human flourishing, particularly among the working class. Aesthetically minded pundits love to champion the virtues of densely packed neighborhoods, with their efficient use of space and their gorgeous mosaics of diversity, and there's no question that the new urbanism is a vast improvement over the massive housing projects and inhuman towers that dominated urban planning in the 1960s and 1970s. But if you're looking for the kind of social capital that keeps Sam's Club voters above water, the suburbs are actually a better bet. As a recent study by Jan Brueckner and Ann Largey notes, Americans who live in lower-density—that is, more suburban—neighborhoods have more friends overall, are more likely to spend time with their neighbors, and are more likely to belong to local clubs or social groups than their urban counterparts. The study suggests several explanations: Cities offer more distractions, which may make neighborliness less important to one's social life; overcrowding may lead people to "draw inward"; and high urban crime rates may erode trust among neighbors.

This phenomenon dovetails with the research of Robert Putnam, the sociologist who first coined the term "bowling alone" to describe America's declining social capital. In a large-scale study that he at first deemed too depressing to publish, Putnam found that too much diversity kills off civic cooperation and increases mistrust—of neighbors, newspapers, and local government. ("It's not just that we don't trust people who are not like us," Putnam has remarked. "In diverse communities, we don't trust people who do look like us.") It flies in the face of forty years of *bienpensant* assumptions, but movement from crowded urban areas to the suburbs and exurbs might be a great boon to America's civic life, and government shouldn't stand in its way.

What do these realities mean for public policy? In cities, it means that a Sam's Club agenda would seek to improve the stock of affordable housing for parents with children by fighting development policies that privilege childless singles and wealthy rentiers. In the suburbs and exurbs, it means that politicians should back attempts to rebuild and expand America's transportation infrastructure, which currently provides a literal roadblock to working-class voters who want both good jobs and affordable housing. In both places, it means confronting the zoning restrictions and onerous environmental regulations designed to keep property values high and privilege existing homeowners over aspiring ones.

The modern commute, in particular, should be a target of profamily outrage. As Nicholas Kulish of the *New York Times* has pointed out, twenty-five years ago the average American spent just sixteen hours annually sitting in traffic; by 2003, the last year for which statistics are available, the typical commuter was losing forty-seven hours to congestion, at a cost of $63.1 billion (and 2.3 billion extra gallons of gasoline burned) per annum. America's highway infrastructure simply hasn't been modernized sufficiently to keep up with population growth—vehicle-lane miles traveled have increased by nearly 150 percent since the 1970s, but America has added a mere 5 percent in highway capacity—putting an immense strain on working parents' schedules, pocketbooks, and tempers. Naturally, the problem is likely to get worse; in *The Road More Traveled*, their manifesto for a saner transportation policy, Ted Balaker and Sam Staley estimate that traffic delays will increase by another 65 percent over the next quarter century.

Liberals generally insist that the traffic problem can be alleviated only by pushing commuters onto mass transit (which has largely flopped as a solution to congestion in most regions), because building more highways "induces demand" and leaves the roads just as congested as before. But as Balaker and Staley note, increasing pavement reliably reduces commuting delays: Dallas has twice as much pavement per person as Los Angeles, and (surprise!) half the congestion. And more lanes are just the beginning of the search for creative solutions: Private-public partnerships, in which toll highways are administered by companies with an interest in maximizing movement through their toll booths, can provide needed funds for infrastructure; traffic signal patterns can be optimized and freeway ramps metered to keep the flow of traffic steady throughout a commute; and differential pricing on lanes and highways can reduce congestion by drawing more commuters into off-peak hours.

The last solution will require a shift toward flexible work schedules, but this is already happening in many industries, and it brings us to another pro-family response to the commuting dilemma—telecommuting, that is, one of the great boons of the Internet age, which as many as 44 million Americans already do part-time. Working long-distance, whether you're a well-off lawyer or a working-class data processor with a degree from the local technical school, promises not only to shore up family life—by enabling parents to live in cheaper areas and spend more time with their children—but to reduce our economy's environmental footprint into the bargain. Best of all, expanding telecommuting would be both pro-family and pro-growth: As Walter Russell Mead has pointed out, the "average American worker spends about one hour per day commuting to and from work—the equivalent of six full workweeks a year," and therefore "someone who telecommutes one day a week saves the equivalent of one work week a year."

Moreover, as Mead argues, a large-scale investment in a flexible, disaster-proof telecommuting infrastructure makes sense as a national security measure, to help the country cope with everything from a terrorist attack to a hurricane. Today's commuters rely on Eisenhower's interstate highway system, which was originally built to ensure the rapid movement of troops and supplies during the Cold War; tomorrow's could similarly depend on a world-class telecommuting infrastructure sponsored by the Department of Homeland Security.

The Health Care Dilemma

No working-class political movement can succeed, though, unless it makes a push for reform in what may be the greatest source of anxiety for working families: the country's health-care system. Americans consistently rank health care as among the most pressing issues facing the country—far ahead of Social Security and eclipsed only by the threat of terrorism and the war in Iraq. In a way, this is a puzzle, since those same voters regularly pronounce themselves satisfied with their own health care. In a recent Kaiser Family Foundation study, nearly 90 percent of those surveyed pronounced themselves content with the quality of care they receive. The explanation, predictably, has to do with growing insecurity: People like the health care they get, but they're worried they won't keep getting it.

By now, the fact that over 46 million Americans are uninsured is familiar. Conservatives rightly note that many of these millions are uninsured by choice: A third of the uninsured are eligible for programs like Medicaid but fail to sign up, and another fifth, many of them young and healthy, choose not to buy coverage even though they make over $50,000 a year. This suggests that the problem of the constantly uninsured isn't as dire as liberals sometimes make it out to be, which is true enough—but it's also true that the 46 million figure is a snapshot, the number who are uninsured at a particular moment in time. The number of Americans who are uninsured *at some point* during a typical year—usually because they lose coverage while switching jobs—ranges from 57 million to 69 million. Over a period of twenty-four months, that number climbs to over 80 million.

Meanwhile, millions of children lack medical coverage. This means that at some point every two years, millions of American parents dread seeing their child catch a bad flu for fear of facing long lines at an understaffed, overworked emergency room. Even if this transitional period lasts only a few months, it's a period fraught with anxiety. And the cost of care keeps going up. Premiums have increased by over 70 percent since 2000 for roughly the same quality of care, while structural changes to the

American economy make matters worse. As employment shifts from large to small firms, job-based coverage has been in steep decline. Health insurance premiums are growing far faster than wages—as much as five times as fast—and smaller employers are having a particularly hard time keeping up. As you'd expect, the decline has been sharpest of all among the poor and near-poor, particularly in Southern states. Between 2000 and 2004, the number of uninsured climbed by 6 million. That number would have been higher by 9 million had the government not stepped in with patchwork efforts to cover children. These interventions have made a major difference, but they've also created a bizarre and tragic situation in which families are divided against themselves, between health-care haves and have-nots.

Both Right and Left have their preferred narratives of what to do about health care. On the Right, the answer is more market efficiency: Costs are going up, conservatives argue, because prices aren't transparent and employer-provided plans subsidize far more health-care consumption than is necessary. Thus initiatives like the Health Savings Account (HSA), a favorite of the Bush administration, which replaces traditional insurance with the combination of a high-deductible policy to cover catastrophic expenses and a tax-free savings account that can be used to cover routine health-care costs. The idea is to give individuals the same tax breaks that employers get in purchasing health-insurance plans and to encourage people to think like thrifty consumers when they decide whether to visit the doctor. On the Left, the answer is—as it always is—national health care, usually envisioned not as a British-style system, in which the government runs hospitals and pays doctors, but rather as a Canada-style program, in which the government takes over the role of the insurance companies and uses substantial tax increases to cover medical care for everyone.

The trouble with the current conservative answer is that it would likely drive down costs for most people but drive them up for the most vulnerable Americans—the poor and the old, who would be stuck in ever-more-costly traditional plans while the young and the healthy flooded into HSAs. (Many on the Right also overestimate even the savviest consumer's ability to navigate America's byzantine health-care landscape; it's easy to comparison-shop when you're buying a car, but it's a lot harder to do the same when you're buying a health-care plan.) The trouble with the liberal answer, meanwhile, is that it is, over the long term, unsustainable.

Take the French health-care system, a model celebrated by many on the Left. There's no question that the average French family receives a higher quality of care than the average American family. Rates of death from heart disease and diabetes are far lower in France, and the same goes for infant mortality. Better still, the French can choose any doctor or specialist—more choice than your average insured American gets from an HMO. The notion that universal health care limits personal choice doesn't hold in France. So what's not to like?

What's not to like is, well, something most Americans would like very much. In France, you never have to worry about paying for medical care. Apart from modest copayments, the government picks up every tab. This means that health-care consumers are almost completely insulated from the cost of medical services. As a result, costs are rising at a rapid clip, despite price controls and stingy government reimbursements for medical services, and even though French doctors make less than a third of what their American counterparts make. These brakes on cost are what keep France's program solvent, and they wouldn't exist if we implemented a similar system in the United States tomorrow. American doctors will never accept French salaries; nor are Americans likely to accept less medical care than they get now if the reduction in care is dictated by a bureaucrat. Moreover, given that we already overconsume health care on a grand scale (the New America Foundation's

Shannon Brownlee estimates that Americans "spend between one fifth and one third of our health care dollars . . . on care that does nothing to improve our health"), implementing a French-style system in the United States tomorrow could be the equivalent of bringing a glutton to an all-you-can-eat buffet. If this sounds harsh, remember that when the government picks up an ever-increasing tab, taxpayers ultimately lose. So do the millions who simply can't get jobs because the tax burden is so high.

This doesn't mean that America doesn't have a lot to learn from the French system, which demonstrates that government can play a more constructive role in a health-care system than you might think from looking at, say, Britain's justly maligned National Health Service. But any health-care reform needs to include market-based mechanisms that will make Americans *more* cost conscious, not less. As Jason Furman of the centrist Hamilton Project points out, in 1965, health spending per capita was $995. By 2006, it had sextupled, reaching $6,640. Out-of-pocket expenditures, by contrast, rose from only $483 to $837. Insulating Americans from the rising cost of health care hasn't been a free lunch: Private insurance and the government have picked up the slack, and that's meant higher premiums and higher taxes. But it's kept most people from having any "skin in the game" where health care is concerned, driving up prices and encouraging unnecessary consumption.

Is it possible to guarantee that all Americans get the health care they need *and* contain costs while preserving the level of market-driven innovation that's arguably the best feature of the present system? Is there a way to steer between Right and Left, cherrypicking the best ideas from both? For now, the bipartisan answer seems to be the kind of universal *private* insurance that a number of states—including Massachusetts and California— are beginning to experiment with. This approach accepts the liberal goal of universal coverage, but instead of approaching reform as the Left does, as a problem for the uninsured—a matter of charity for those less fortunate—it casts the health-care crisis as a problem for the *insured*, for people whose insurance plans will lapse if they lose or shift jobs, and who must pay extra, in the form of higher premiums, to cover the medical bills of the permanently uninsured. With this in mind, Republican governors like Mitt Romney and Arnold Schwarzenegger have tried to make health insurance universal by making it *mandatory*. The political message is appealing to the partisans of self-reliance: Allowing individuals to forgo coverage encourages the young and healthy to live dangerously, giving them a free ride on the public purse when things go awry and making health care more expensive for everyone else. If you expect government to step in when the going gets tough, you have an obligation to make a contribution.

Can a system like this work for the nation as a whole? A number of Democrats and Republicans, led by Senators Ron Wyden of Oregon and Bob Bennett of Utah, believe the answer is yes. Unfortunately, it's not even clear that this system can work in Massachusetts and California. Once again, it all comes down to costs. As with the French system, mandating the purchase of insurance does little or nothing to reduce overconsumption. There's no question that moving closer to universal coverage through mandates could generate some savings over time by reducing cost shifting and expanding the market for private health plans. The danger is that all of these gains would be swamped if health-care costs keep rising (and absent any mechanism to drive them down, there's no reason they won't), at which point the pressure to increase subsidies will be irresistible. Rising subsidies will in turn lead to further increased costs, and so on in an endless spiral. As with traditional single-payer systems, significant rationing will become inevitable as other government functions are crowded out.

So what would a more sustainable health-care reform package look like? It should guarantee that no family will ever be at economic risk due to necessary medical expenses, and it should maintain a strong free-market element, encouraging families to choose medical services that offer value for money. We could reach these goals through a series of incremental reforms, which keep employer-based coverage mostly intact, or we could go for a more dramatic break with the past. Let's start with the politically safe route.

Because most Americans are happy with the coverage provided by their employers, an obvious health-care reform strategy is to make it easier—that is, cheaper—for employers to provide insurance. The easiest way to reduce the cost of coverage would be for the federal government to help pay for, or "reinsure," the most expensive patients, a proposal that Bill Frist floated during his tenure as Senate Majority Leader and which has drawn intermittent bipartisan support ever since. Under a federal reinsurance program, the government would step in as soon as costs exceed a certain level: If a cancer patient spends more than $50,000, for example, the government would take on some share of any additional expenditures. (A striking number to keep in mind is that roughly *four*-fifths of all medical expenditures can be attributed to *one*-fifth of all patients.) This means all Americans—not just the employees of a particular company—would share the burden of paying for health care for the unlucky few. As a result, employers would no longer fear hiring an employee who has a daughter with a chronic illness, and insurance companies would have less reason to discriminate against high-risk patients. This would be a particular boon to small businesses and old industrial companies like General Motors, which have been crippled by the health-care costs generated by aging and ailing retired workers.

To make sure that these reinsurance costs don't spiral out of control, Stuart Altman of Brandeis University has proposed that insurers be required to use a case management system for catastrophic cases and to limit wasteful care; the government would pay no more than 75 percent of costs above the catastrophic level, to discourage insurers from running up costs. To control costs *below* the level where reinsurance kicks in, reformers might adopt Jason Furman's plan for "progressive cost-sharing," under which Medicare and Medicaid would be required—and insurance companies incentivized—to have patients pay half of all medical expenses out-of-pocket up to, say, an average of 7.5 percent of income, with the very poor paying nothing at all and wealthier families paying somewhat more. If implemented across the health-care system, across public programs and private insurers, Furman believes that cost-sharing could reduce total health-spending and health-care premiums alike by as much as one-third, savings that would more than make up for the additional out-of-pocket expenditures.

Another incremental measure that would help control costs would be to reduce the current tax deduction for employer-provided health coverage or replace it with a flat credit that applies irrespective of income. Right now, the $200 billion we spend annually in federal subsidies for employment-based health insurance provides the most help to those who need it least by encouraging companies to spend far more than they otherwise would on gold-plated plans for their best-paid employees, driving up overall costs for everyone else. (According to one estimate, high-income households are subsidized to the tune of $4,000 while low-income households receive only $1,000 in tax benefits.) Limiting the deduction to $11,500 for a family plan and $5,000 for individuals—an amount that matches the average annual premiums—or replacing it with a flat credit would save the public money and increase cost-consciousness among well-off Americans. The rich would still be free to purchase insurance above and beyond what the deduction or credit covers, but the federal government wouldn't be subsidizing them.

Taken together with a Medicaid reform that expands eligibility while cracking down on overspending, these proposals would reduce costs, maintain or even increase the role of the free market, and move us closer to universal coverage without causing too much disruption. But such an incremental approach is far from perfect, and its weaknesses may prove fatal if new medical innovations make it cheap and easy to identify the genes that make us more or less susceptible to all kinds of chronic (and expensive) illnesses. Such advances are very good news, obviously, insofar as they will make it easier for us to fight disease. Yet they will also sharpen the conflict between private insurers, who through no malice want to keep costs down, and the insured, who want to be cared for when they need it most. A world where insurance companies know, to the percentage point, your odds of getting cancer or heart disease, may be a world where conservatives as well as liberals find themselves looking for ways to reduce the role that private insurance companies play in our health-care system.

Brad DeLong, an economist at the University of California, Berkeley, has sketched out a road map—"an unrealistic, impractical, utopian plan," he humbly calls it—that aims to do exactly that. Under the DeLong Plan, the government would require all individuals and families to set aside 15 percent of income in a Health Savings Account. During the course of a year, you use your HSA to pay medical expenses. As soon as you've run out, the government steps in to cover all additional costs, without the insurer-as-middleman approach of a reinsurance system. Any money that you don't spend either rolls over into a retirement account or is returned to you in the form of a tax refund.

Insurance companies wouldn't disappear under such a system, but they would become optional. All transactions below the 15 percent ceiling would be subject to the free play of market forces, with individuals contracting with medical providers for the best, most cost-effective care. Some people might contract with an insurance provider to prepay for medical services. Most would skip that step and go straight to their family physician.

Does this represent a federal takeover of health care? Hardly. It's important to keep in mind that the government's role in health care is vast under the status quo—but government involvement is masked through the tax system, and government largesse is channeled disproportionately toward those who need it least. The DeLong Plan would instead focus government resources on those who need it most *when* they need it most. It would require slightly higher tax rates, but it would mean higher take-home pay as well, since health-insurance premiums would pass into history. By freeing consumers and providers alike from the complexities and distortions of the insurance marketplace, and by relieving businesses of the cost of maintaining miniature welfare states, it would create a health-care marketplace that's arguably *more* laissez-faire than the current hodgepodge of capitalism and command-and-control. And such a reform would open the way for a broader attack on anticompetitive practices in the health-care sector.

At present, the most powerful players in the medical marketplace do everything in their power to suppress free, open, and fair competition. Populist outrage at medical-industrial complex profiteering has mainly been directed at pharmaceutical companies. But as professors Michael Porter and Elizabeth Teisberg have argued, the entire health-care industry is designed to reduce costs borne by intermediaries—hospitals, health plans, physicians' groups—rather than to increase value for patients. There is a relentless drive to shift costs onto individuals and to minimize competition through network restrictions that prevent consumers from finding the best care. The lack of information concerning medical outcomes, for instance, is an obvious scandal. Without the ability to measure the quality of medical care, it's almost impossible to discern whether or not our money is being wasted. In today's system, insurers and medical providers collude to suppress information about the quality of care, a practice that would be considered intolerable in any other industry. Meanwhile, by negotiating for steep discounts from provider groups, large employers and the government make the individual insurance market intolerably expensive for small businesses and individuals.

Eliminating these bottlenecks will, over time, go a long way toward reducing costs and increasing consumer choice. Prices will become more transparent, and they will be based on the nature and complexity of the service rather than the imperatives of insurance plans. Providers will be more likely to charge for a bundle of services relating to a particular condition or episode of care, not each discrete test, and more likely to set a single price in advance. A sensible provider will then do everything possible to keep costs down for all comers, rather than run up the bill by calling for unnecessary tests. A more empirical sensibility is likely to result. Procedures that work will slowly crowd out those that don't.

Naturally, some will bridle at the kind of case management that the government would need to use, under DeLong's proposal, to hold down costs for those patients whose medical bills exceed 15 percent of income. But Americans will be free to rely on private care instead, provided they are willing to pay for it. Rather than fall back on the government for catastrophic coverage, they can instead contract with elite private insurers, which will deliver experimental technologies and extraordinary amenities. Eventually, the private insurers that win loyal customers among upper-income Americans will most likely be integrated health-care plans like Kaiser Permanente and Intermountain Healthcare, which use evidence-based medicine to deliver a higher quality of care at (again) a lower cost. This segment of the new medical marketplace will drive innovation by providing an outlet for daring and untested approaches.

Meanwhile, all of these reforms would have salutary effects on family life. Severing health-care coverage from employment would eliminate the gaps in coverage that occur when workers move from one job to the next. Workers will no longer be shackled to jobs they despise, thus offering a tremendous boon to productivity. More important, if your coverage were portable, you'd feel more secure in moving your family to a community with a lower cost of living, or where you're more likely to find remunerative employment. At the same time, making health care more universal and affordable would reduce the costs of child rearing, encouraging family formation and improving family stability.

Creating such a system might not be politically feasible. But in an age of anxiety, health-care reform is an obvious opportunity for the Right to demonstrate that market-friendly solutions can actually increase economic security rather than reduce it. And given that the likely alternative is a turn toward a European-style single-payer system, conservatives have every reason to strive to make a more flexible, market-oriented, *American* vision a reality.

The Taxman Cometh

Finally, a family-friendly agenda needs to address the issue of taxes. For thirty years, the heart of Republican political success has been tax cuts. By embracing steep rate reductions, President Reagan made a decisive break with decades of defeatist fiscal orthodoxy. Instead of depressing squabbles over how to slice a shrinking pie, the GOP offered the vision of a thriving entrepreneurial economy. But like aging hippies who never quite got over Woodstock, many of those young Reaganites, now safely ensconced in the GOP establishment, view income tax cuts as a permanent ticket to political power—even though the working class isn't buying what they're selling.

Just before the Reagan tax cuts, a median-income four-person family paid about 12 percent of their total income in federal income taxes. Reducing that burden, predictably enough, yielded a political windfall for Republicans. But over the intervening years, the burden borne by these voters has sharply decreased. Today, the bite the federal income tax takes out of working-class and middle-class paychecks stands at roughly *half* the pre-Reagan level. The American taxpayer still has plenty to complain about: State and local taxes have kept on increasing, and the same goes for the payroll tax, the most unfair and destructive tax on the books. But the federal income tax, the great bête noire of tax-cutting conservatives, is no longer Middle America's worst nightmare. (That distinction belongs to your unfriendly neighborhood health insurance company and the folks who set your property taxes.) It's hardly surprising that political support for tax cuts has diminished markedly, as working class voters weigh the costs and benefits of government spending and increasingly find that they're coming out ahead.

What *is* surprising is that so many Republicans keep behaving, despite all evidence to the contrary, like we're still living in 1980. Every Republican wants to be Ronald Reagan running against tax-and-spend Jimmy Carter, but Jimmy Carter has long since left the building. Democrats nationwide have learned how to talk about taxes the hard way, which is why they increasingly focus on tax fairness and delivering high-quality public services. That's why Republicans, even in states as Red as Virginia, are losing the argument over taxes and spending. To win the argument, they need reforms that meet the real needs of families.

What would a sweeping pro-family tax reform look like? For one thing, it would keep taxes lowest for those entering the workforce and preparing to have children and for young families making investments in their offspring. As workers gain experience and enter their peak earning years, it makes sense for the tax burden to increase. Ramesh Ponnuru's plan, which we discussed at the outset of this chapter, would be one way to achieve this effect, and it has the virtue of being more politically realistic than the more radical alternatives. But it's worth considering another, still bolder choice—making a frontal assault on the payroll tax.

When you think about why voters are less enamored of tax cuts than they used to be, consider that the biggest tax most working-class Americans pay is one that nobody even considers cutting. The theory behind the payroll tax, or FICA, is simple: Over the course of our working lives, we make "contributions" to Social Security and Medicare—*mandatory* contributions, of course—and eventually we get our money's worth in the form of old-age pensions and medical care well into our dotage. The truth, of course, is rather different. Social Security and Medicare are "pay-as-you-go," with today's workers paying for today's retirees, and the system is enormously regressive, since workers making more than $94,200 pay nothing into the Social Security system above that threshold. This financing scheme made a certain sense in an era of relative economic equality; today, in a less egalitarian era, it's increasingly perverse. Not only does the payroll tax fail to mitigate inequality, but it actually *reinforces* it.

The obvious way to address this imbalance is to means-test Social Security, a proposal that many reformers, Right and Left, have long embraced as a way to keep the program solvent. Means-testing is a good idea, but it redresses the regressiveness of the payroll tax at the back end; a better idea would be to reduce the bite that the payroll tax takes out of working-class incomes in the first place. Kenneth Scheve, a political scientist at Yale, and Matthew J. Slaughter, an economist at Dartmouth, recently proposed eliminating the payroll tax entirely for workers making less than the median income, a tax cut that would increase after-tax income for working families by $3,800, an amount that would make a tremendous difference for strapped Sam's Club voters. Their proposal, which would be funded by either raising the cap or making the payroll tax rate progressive, might be too radical a departure from the "everybody pays" ethos of Social Security to succeed. More feasible, perhaps, would be a push to *reduce*, rather than eliminate, payroll taxes for low- and middle-income families, and make up for the lost revenue by means-testing benefits. Taken on its own, such a measure would be an ideal way for conservatives to once again make tax cuts appealing in Middle America; as part of a renewed push for Social Security reform, it would provide a populist sweetener to the fiscal belt-tightening necessary to keep the program solvent.

The ideal course, however, would be to give up completely on the illusion that Social Security is something other than pay-as-you-go, and scrap the payroll tax entirely and pay for old-age insurance out of general revenue.

This would require a dramatic increase in income taxes, of course, since the payroll tax currently raises $760 billion, almost as much as the $1.1 trillion raised by the federal income tax. Unless, that is, we then took the still-bolder step of replacing the payroll tax *and* the federal income tax with a progressive consumption tax, in which workers would be taxed on the difference between their income and their savings. Overall levels of taxation would remain roughly the same, but incentives for work and investment would be supercharged.

Obviously, this would have to be a long-range goal for a Sam's Club majority, not an immediate objective. But the benefits of a consumption tax would be considerable. It would reward people for saving and investing early in life. It would hit the idle rich—affluent retirees drawing down their savings, trust fund babies buying penthouse apartments—hardest, while the productive rich, and their income from investments and business ventures, would emerge considerably less scathed. Its progressivity would appeal to liberals, while the pro-growth Right, and the business community, would embrace its simplicity and its favorable treatment of savings and investment.

Meanwhile, the exemptions, deductions, and rebates that make the system progressive would be chosen with the interests of the American family uppermost in mind. A generous personal deduction, and of course a generous child tax credit, would protect working-class parents. Then there are all the other tax deductions—for state and local taxes, charitable contributions, home mortgages, employer-provided health care, and so forth—that riddle the tax code. A Sam's Club conservatism would pick and choose from this list, targeting deductions to key constituencies. We have already argued that the deduction for employer-provided health care should be reduced or eliminated. The home mortgage deduction could be limited to low-income couples and families with children—after all, it hardly makes sense for the government to be subsidizing the McMansions of childless dual-income families. Taking a page from President Bush's tax-overhaul panel, state and local tax exemptions could easily be axed—and the subsequent revenue enhancement used to finance measures to help child-rearing families when they need it most (with deductions for college, health care, and the like).

Admittedly, there would be losers from such a reform. Affluent, childless couples and middle-aged singles would undoubtedly face stiffer rates, as would the wealthy residents of high-tax states. But the majority of Americans would benefit greatly—particularly working-class voters, who would have the reform to thank for lower, simpler taxes. And such a reform would disproportionately benefit the most productive Americans: bold upper-class entrepreneurs, thrifty blue-collar workers, the upwardly mobile poor.

Above all, like all of the reforms we've proposed, it would benefit parents with children—the people making the most significant investment possible in the American future and the people most deserving of government support.

8

Up from Compassion

In the early 1990s, an anthropologist named Katherine Newman conducted interviews with three hundred men and
women who were applying for work at a fast-food restaurant in
Harlem. Two hundred of Newman's subjects were hired by the
chain; the other hundred were turned down. The lucky ones
were paid minimum wage to be abused by customers and mis-
treated by managers in a line of work that offered little chance
for advancement. The unlucky remained unemployed, adrift in
the post-Reagan recession, seemingly trapped in the hopeless
lot of the working poor.

In 2006, Newman published *Chutes and Ladders*, her second study of her interview subjects' progress over the decade-
plus since. As you might expect, many of the forty she tracked
down—roughly a third, by Newman's count—were still stagnating, either unemployed or laboring at minimum-wage jobs. But
nearly a quarter of her seemingly hopeless subjects were "high
flyers" making over $15 an hour—success stories that included
"Adam," a high-school dropout who is currently a driver for a
delivery company, earning $70,000 a year; or "Ebony," who
went from flipping burgers to working as a law firm receptionist

and attending college at night; or "Kyesha," who has a union job as a janitor for the New York Housing Authority.

Most accounts of underclass poverty, Newman notes, focus on the gulf between the poor and the rest of American society, and the anti-work, anti-advancement "oppositional culture" that afflicts underclass life. But in her interviews, she found that most of her subjects had more in common with their socioeconomic betters than she had expected. On matters of work and welfare, she noted, they were often "closer to a conservative, 'red state' perspective than the liberal, 'blue state' view that most sociologists, myself included, subscribe to." Even those who had been on welfare expressed a negative attitude toward government handouts and the people who accept them, and faith in the power of the individual to shape his or her own destiny. As Paul Tough put it, reviewing *Chutes and Ladders* in the *New York Times Book Review*, the "system really is sometimes rigged against these workers, and they know it. But despite all this, they speak persuasively and passionately about the way work, even rotten work, gives meaning to their lives. Stories like Adam's and Ebony's only confirm to them what they already believe: that anyone can succeed if they work hard enough."

Newman's book is a look at a particular and not necessarily representative group of women and men, but it suggests an important truth about poverty in the United States—namely, that there isn't a bright line dividing the poor from the rest of the working class, either economically or culturally. High-school graduates with steady jobs can lose them and slip down into poverty; high-school dropouts can work their way out of the inner city and claim their share of the suburban dream. Which means, in turn, that an agenda aimed at improving the fortunes of the Sam's Club demographic needs to be attuned to poverty as well as insecurity. It needs to address the needs not only of parents struggling to stay together, but of people who never have the chance to form families in the first place.

Respect, Not Compassion

In the early 1990s, an alliance of conservatives and neoliberals joined forces to reform welfare, ignoring the objections and fearmongering of nearly everyone to their left. A decade later, this reform stands as working-class conservatism's most impressive domestic policy achievement to date. Unlike so many "reforms" that all too predictably change things for the worse—the McCain-Feingold campaign finance bill is the most obvious recent example—the renovation of welfare delivered exactly what it promised: reduced welfare rolls and increased employment rates.

Since then, though, conservatives have shied away from dramatic efforts to improve the lot of the underclass. In electoral terms, this is understandable and predictable. The poor aren't exactly reliable Republican voters, and the sense of crisis—ever-rising crime rates, an obviously broken welfare system—that spurred action in the early 1990s has largely evaporated. But there's certainly room for reforms that would help Americans escape from poverty into self-sufficiency and upward mobility. Despite its success in reducing teen pregnancy and putting welfare recipients to work, for instance, welfare reform has done little to reverse the collapse in marriage rates among the working poor or arrest the growth of illegitimacy and child poverty. Conservatives and neoliberals have fought hard to eliminate perverse incentives that discourage marriage, but the dire shortage of marriageable men in poor communities is a far more serious problem. Exhorting single mothers to find husbands, and prospective husbands to enter the workforce, can do only so much good when the least-educated men, those without high-school diplomas, continue to see their wages stagnate or decline—and when so many end up incarcerated.

A Sam's Club politics has to revolve around self-reliance and self-help. But among the very poor, the obstacles to bootstrapping your way upward remain formidable. President Bush recognized this by calling for a more "compassionate conservatism," which would refuse, as he put it, to "balance the budget on the backs of the poor." But while his instincts were sound, the language of compassion strikes the wrong note. It speaks to upper-middle-class empathy, not to the aspirations of poor Americans with the drive to succeed. For a generation, anti-poverty campaigns have fallen into this trap too often, emphasizing pity over self-help, framing government interventions in terms of charitable outreach, and poor-mouthing the prospects of the very people they set out to help. In the process, they have created an assumption that the poorest Americans simply aren't capable of the kind of drive, ambition, and zeal for self-improvement that defines the American character.

In place of this mix of pity and condescension, we need an expanded self-improvement agenda, with less emphasis on warm sentiments and more on offering tools that help the Adams and Kyeshas of the world advance toward prosperity. The Earned Income Tax Credit (EITC) has been a great success in this regard, and expanding it would do far more to help the working poor than hiking the minimum wage. But the EITC is indirect, requiring workers to apply to the IRS for their money, which means that many workers don't lay claim to it, and this makes it a less-than-ideal spur to lure idle young men into the workforce. As Mickey Kaus has put it: "It's much more important for unskilled young men to hear 'They're hiring right now over at Home Depot for $10 an hour' than 'If you manage to find an employer willing to hire you . . . and then you apply to the IRS you'll someday get a few hundred dollars back.' If everyone had long time horizons we wouldn't have a ghetto-poverty problem."

To make that ten-dollar-an-hour job a live possibility, one tool that's worth considering is a program of wage subsidies, like that proposed by Columbia University economist Edmund

Phelps, which would help less-educated single men with low-paying jobs make ends meet, thereby making them more desirable marriage partners. Given the right boost, poor young men could become working-class fathers. While the Left bashes Wal-Mart, which creates more jobs and more savings for non–college-educated workers than a million pressure groups, wage subsidies would recognize that low-wage employers aren't the enemy when it comes to fighting poverty. By working with these employers—instead of imposing higher pay by fiat, as a minimum-wage increase would do—conservatives can deliver results where most populist programs are likely to fail and make inroads among low-income strivers on their way to the middle class.

Far from being a new entitlement, wage subsidies would be an anti-entitlement, with government helping only those who are already helping themselves. Unlike more complicated interventions, they would fulfill the wise libertarian dictum that one of the few things that government can be counted on to do efficiently and well is write checks. There's no question that a serious wage subsidy would be expensive—Phelps figures up to $85 billion a year—but this money might come back to the public purse in the form of lower incarceration rates and reduced outlays of other government benefits. And such a program could be funded in the short run by cuts in benefits to those who are fit to work and don't—thus increasing the incentives for holding down a job and raising a family, and leaving shirkers at the mercy of family and friends, or private charity.

Consider that the U.S. currently spends roughly $500 billion a year on a host of overlapping welfare programs, almost none of which have as much promise as avenues for advancement rather than dependency. At present, many of the Tommy Thompson–style reforms of the 1990s languish half-implemented. More than a dozen states, for instance, have never enforced the 1996 reform's requirement that they actually kick people off the rolls if they refuse to even try to find a job. In New York City, a relative success story, 46 percent of recipients who have been ordered to look for work refuse to comply, and the city is largely powerless to force them. Streamlining welfare doesn't mean giving up on the hopeless cases, but it does mean doing a far better job separating out the small minority who can't live without government assistance from the vast majority who can, given the right incentives. The Bush administration, in one of its few poverty-fighting successes, has backed policies that place the most dysfunctional 10 to 20 percent of the homeless population—the hard cases, the drug addicts and lunatics who are often massive financial burdens for their local shelters, jails, and hospitals—into permanent "supportive" housing, with access to medical and counseling services. By singling out this small group and lavishing resources on them, localities are driving down their homelessness rate, and actually saving money overall. It's a model that should be widely imitated: more help for those who desperately need it, and strictly temporary help for those who don't, to push them off the dole and into the workforce.

But keeping young men in the workforce also means keeping them in school and giving them the basic skills they need to keep a job. Skills beget skills: We can try to address skill deficits through remedial education and worker retraining later in life, but beyond a certain age habits and expectations are very difficult to change. With this in mind, we need to consider radical experiments with the structure of public education, both in the poorest parts of the country and nationwide.

School Choice for All

Stable family life depends on economic security, but it depends on good schools as well. When Sam's Club voters pack up and move to the exurbs, they aren't just looking for cheaper, bigger homes—they're looking for better kindergartens and high schools. Unfortunately, rather than attracting parents through their quality of instruction, suburban districts attract parents through their quality of *exclusion*—specifically, the extent to which the school in question excludes poor children, students from single-parent families, and kids with special needs. This dismal picture is yet another factor in the decline of social mobility that we described in Chapter 6. Now it's time to offer an alternative.

The obvious conservative solution to this problem is school choice, but the push for vouchers has run into steep resistance everywhere it's been tried—from the public school bureaucracy, of course, but also from suburban voters who fear, understandably, that school choice will open up their schools to children from the communities they left behind, trailing chaos in their wake. The political impediments to implementing vouchers shouldn't prevent conservatives from continuing to push for them, but they suggest a need for alternate avenues as well.

Here's one path to reform that right-wingers might consider championing. When conservatives laud the virtues of school choice, reformist liberals tend to respond by lauding public charter schools, which free individual institutions from the various constraints imposed by their districts—particularly the onerous labor contracts. Conventional public schools have to abide by spending formulas and staffing ratios set by a central board of education. In big cities, this means that bureaucrats downtown settle on how much money will be spent on teachers, teachers' aides, textbooks, and just about everything else. Local management—that is, the principal who knows the situation close at hand—has relatively little discretion. Charter schools, by contrast, allow principals to be innovative and entrepreneurial, allocating funds and making hiring decisions to address the immediate needs of their schools, rather than to satisfy the dictates of the bureaucracy.

But the success of charter schools breeds resentment as well as admiration. It's no surprise that administrators and teachers in conventional public schools are annoyed by the attention lavished on charters. If they had the same freedom, they argue, they could achieve and exceed charter school results. So why not give it to them? Instead of slowly expanding the number of public charter schools, why not offer the same spending discretion to *every* public school?

This sounds like a political pipe dream that couldn't possibly make it past entrenched school bureaucracies and teachers' unions. But consider one city where the idea has already been put into practice—San Francisco, that citadel of raging public-sector liberalism. Apart from a small amount of money for a principal and one clerical assistant, all funds that go to San Francisco public schools are allocated according to a "weighted student formula." The more students you attract, the more money you get. Not all students count for the same amount of money, of course. Poor children are entitled to a bit more, and students with disabilities are entitled to a lot more to account for higher costs. This means that schools have a powerful incentive to enroll the kinds of students traditional public schools prefer to shunt aside. To attract students, schools have to differentiate themselves. As some programs, particularly foreign-language immersion programs, have grown popular, more seats have been added to meet demand.

What would happen if the weighted student formula spread across the country? At the very least we'd see a sharp decline in corruption, as centralized spending decisions, fat targets for self-dealing, dissipate in favor of transparent spending decisions made at the local level. When a few million dollars vanish downtown, the culprits and consequences are difficult to pinpoint. When $10,000 goes missing in a weighted student formula school, it's coming out of some teacher's paycheck. More important, we'd eventually see a dizzying variety of educational programs tailored to meet the needs of a constantly changing student population. Principals attuned to the needs of their students would thrive, and their schools would steadily expand. Provided the regulations aren't too stifling, a successful principal might even franchise her school by farming out her devoted disciples to run clones in other neighborhoods and even other cities. Schools that fail to take advantage of their newfound freedom would, over time, be forced to shut their doors, freeing resources for better schools elsewhere. Better still, poor kids, who will have the most money strapped to their backs, would attract the most attention from entrepreneurial principals eager to expand their bailiwick.

The weighted student formula wouldn't just increase the scope of choice and competition. It would also effectively sidestep the traditional liberal-conservative debate over education. By leaving district boundaries and funding more or less intact for purposes of administrative convenience while encouraging experimentation within each district, the weighted student formula could allay suburbanites' fears while delivering many of the benefits of a voucher program.

But in areas where poverty is deeply entrenched, this kind of reform might not go far enough. Desperate situations call for sweeping experiments. For instance, given the potential benefits of early childhood interventions, and the limits to what can be accomplished with older children, some schools might experiment with beginning pre-secondary schooling at age three and ending it at age sixteen, as a recent report from the New Commission on the Skills of the American Workforce recommended, with either college or some kind of vocational training to follow. There should also be more experiments with staggered school years, in which holiday breaks are expanded and summer vacations dramatically reduced. One of the main culprits behind increasing educational inequality appears to be that old standby of American childhood, summer vacation. It turns out that poor kids make steady gains throughout the school year, even in the lowest-performing schools. Over the summer months, while middle-class and affluent children have a wide array of enriching experiences, the poor lose ground, sometimes dramatically. The cumulative effect is to widen an already wide educational gap. If we could hold the line and eliminate summer learning loss, we could start the process of closing that gap, and the beneficial effects would ripple from one generation to the next.

The Hamilton Project has suggested tackling summer learning loss with a program of Summer Opportunity Scholarships (SOS), which would give poor elementary-school students a voucher to pay for a six-week summer enrichment program. The idea is that by taking part in a program focused on basic skills, these programs will mimic the educational reinforcement that occurs naturally in better-off families. Because SOS is a voucher program, it would allow for a wide range of providers, including churches and for-profit groups, and a fair bit of experimentation.

A truly transformative program, however, would reach beyond families in poverty to include the broader working class. It's easy to see why many Sam's Club voters might object to a program like SOS, which benefits only poor children, particularly when so many find it difficult to care for their own children during long summer vacations. A more inclusive program would be far more expensive, to be sure, but it would provide educational benefits to families that are often only one or two steps removed from poverty and prevent their children from slipping down into the underclass. By meeting the needs of more families, it would rest on a more robust political foundation. And by accustoming parents to school choice, it might provide an entering wedge for the broader voucherization that conservatives have long sought.

Most important, perhaps, it would be more likely to have a transformative effect on America's growing population of high-school dropouts, enabling them to join the workforce rather than slip into a life of crime. And not a moment too soon: Public order will always be at the heart of any working-class politics, and though lawlessness has receded as a hot-button issue over the last decade, that may be about to change.

Defusing the Crime Bomb

We've already seen, in Chapter 6, how immigration may be producing a rising generation prone to lawbreaking. But there are other factors at work as well, including the unintended consequences of the draconian approach to sentencing and incarceration that helped bring the post-sixties crime wave to an end. Consider that every year approximately 700,000 individuals leave prison, that the vast majority head home to communities that already suffer from high rates of crime and poverty—and that the situation is likely to get worse before it gets better. Huge numbers of prisoners who have been locked up since the 1980s, when tough sentencing spread nationwide, will be released from prison over the next decade. Most of these men were arrested early in life and most had very little in the way of education. Because they entered prison during a particularly punitive time in our history, few of them enjoyed the kinds of opportunities behind bars that are proven to reduce recidivism. Sheer desperation may well drive many of these aging, unskilled men to return to a life of crime.

Unfortunately for the law-abiding, the opportunities for illicit activity are likely to increase just as this generation is hitting the streets. For instance, the illegal drugs that landed many of these men in prison in the first place are being replaced by homegrown drugs that are virtually impossible to interdict. Whereas the process of cultivating opium in Afghanistan or cocaine in Colombia takes a considerable amount of time, crystal meth can be manufactured in any abandoned warehouse or garage from products that are available off the shelf. Transporting heroin or cocaine across international boundaries is a perilous business for all parties involved, but drugs made from household products can be enjoyed in the comfort of one's own home. This new world of drug use *could* largely eliminate the violent crime we associate with the drug trade—no more turf wars, no more shooting galleries in the streets of our major cities—but it's more likely to drive crime rates upward as ill-gotten gains fuel a whole slew of criminal activities, from sex trafficking to armed robbery.

A similar cocktail of demographic change and criminal opportunity led to a crisis of authority in the America of the 1970s, a crisis from which we've yet to fully recover. A new crime wave, particularly one linked to immigration and recidivism, could set us back by decades and lead to renewed racial tension and resentment. And as gang violence spreads beyond the inner cities, Sam's Club voters living in the inner suburbs will find themselves on the front lines. Already, lawbreaking seems poised to be a sleeper issue in the next few election cycles. Violent crime rose in 2005 and 2006, after a decade of decline, and voter anxiety is rising with it: The percentage of Americans who told the General Social Survey that they are "afraid to walk in their neighborhood at night" rose 5 percentage points between 2004 and 2006, after declining steadily every year since 1994.

Instead of simply waiting for a crime explosion, conservatives should find policies to preempt it. The broad-based working-class agenda that we've outlined would play an important role: Wage subsidies could help prevent crime by making legitimate work pay, for instance, and better schools could keep low-income young men out of gangs. Sometimes, though, the best prevention isn't a social program—it's simply having more cops on the beat. It wasn't just prisons, after all, that brought the last crime wave to a halt in the 1990s. It was the dramatic increase in the size of police forces, whose per capita numbers rose by

10 percent between 1994 and 1999, with sharper increases in the biggest cities. And we're still a long way from having a law-enforcement glut: According to an estimate by economist John Donohue, the United States would need to hire 500,000 more police officers before reaching the point of diminishing returns. To put that number in context, there are only 665,000 police officers in the United States at present.

Hiring thousands of new police officers wouldn't just reduce crime—it would create job opportunities for the working class and in particular for young men from inner-city backgrounds. For some, serving in the police could be much like enlisted service in the military. Already, police recruits are often rewarded with educational benefits and home loans; a national program might also give those who've served in the police for, say, five years lifetime access to the Veterans Administration health-care system and other inducements. Joining the police could be an avenue to upward mobility for thousands of young people who can't afford higher education or who simply have a strong desire to serve their communities.

Like a program of wage subsidies, a push to hire more police officers would be populism with a conservative face. Left-wing populists often call for jobs programs to smooth the road up from poverty: John Edwards, for instance, has proposed creating a million new "stepping-stone" jobs at nonprofits or government agencies. But why should we subsidize a new generation of bureaucrats when we can accomplish the same goal by doubling the size of our police departments—and enjoy safer streets?

The Immigration Dilemma

Finally, there's the elephant in the room—immigration itself. Any political agenda tailored to the interest of working-class Americans needs to consider the problem of the influx of low-wage labor from abroad. On the one hand, a country interested in moving poor young men into the workforce would seem to have every reason to limit low-skilled immigration, if not to the minimal levels of the egalitarian 1950s, then at least to a more manageable rate than today's unprecedented influx. As Mickey Kaus has argued, tightening the labor market by reducing competition from abroad is ultimately the only surefire way to help the native-born poor—because employers will often prefer hiring illegal immigrants over, say, young black men, and because only a tight labor market will create wages high enough to lure idlers into the labor force.

But at the same time, no American political movement can afford to treat immigrants, legal or illegal, solely as a threat to the interests of the native born. Immigrants aren't just trespassers; they're future citizens, future voters, and part of an American tradition of aspiration and courage that dates back to the *Arbella*. Mexico isn't just a source of cheap labor, drugs, and destabilizing migrants; it's the ancestral homeland of millions of Americans today and millions more tomorrow. Both political parties have been wary of anti-immigrant sentiment, fearing the taint of nativism and a backlash that could cost them the growing Hispanic vote for a generation or more. This wariness is understandable: Opposition to immigration can shade easily into bigotry, and many of the draconian measures floated on the far Right—like repealing birthright citizenship, or trying to deport illegal immigrants en masse—are pure folly.

But so are policies like the failed "comprehensive" immigration reform of 2007, which in all likelihood would have *increased* the illegal influx, further damaging the economic prospects of low-income native-born workers. Depending on which version passed into law, it would have meant either an amnesty with few strings attached, or worse, a huge class of temporary workers who do the jobs that our own citizens supposedly won't but don't have any chance of becoming citizens themselves. The latter option is not only deeply un-American but a recipe for long-term cultural and economic polarization. (Go ask the Europeans how well their guest-worker programs have been working out lately.)

To avoid these dangers, conservatives need to find common ground between the anti-immigration hawks and the advocates of open borders—by predicating any earned legalization program on increased spending for border control and serious sanctions for employers who hire undocumented workers. Unlike the 1986 attempt at reform, which promised both a crackdown and an amnesty but delivered only the latter, any comprehensive immigration solution needs to demonstrate that it can reduce the immigration rate *before* an earned-legalization program goes into effect; otherwise it will simply become a magnet for still-larger waves of migrants, lured by the prospect of citizenship.

Would a serious crackdown put an end to illegal immigration? Of course not. But it has a better chance of reducing the inflow than many advocates of open borders suggest. Employer sanctions, in particular, haven't been tried and found wanting; they've been found difficult and left untried. In Georgia, which recently passed one of the toughest anti-immigration laws in the nation, raids by federal immigration agents over Labor Day weekend in 2006 cost a chicken-processing company three-quarters of its 900-member workforce. The company insisted that its hometown of Stillmore, Georgia, simply didn't have a large enough workforce to staff the factory, and sure enough, they soon found themselves busing in Laotian Hmong immigrants to fill jobs on the assembly line. But they also started hiring local blacks, with jobs starting at $7 to $9 an hour—a dollar above what they had been paying their illegal workforce—and free transportation and sleeping quarters for those coming in from out of town. And "for the first time in years," the *Wall*

Street Journal noted, the company "aggressively sought workers from the area's state-funded employment office—a key avenue for low-skilled workers to find jobs."

Obviously, these kinds of raids are immensely unpopular with business interests, and they will never be implemented, or continued, without a significant political struggle. (Though again, wage subsidies might help smooth the transition.) But combining such crackdowns with the promise of an eventual earned-legalization program for those already here offers a way forward for politicians who understand the need to limit immigration and control the border but are wary of alienating Hispanic voters with appeals to nativist sentiment. In the long run, the Hispanics who are most likely to vote for the Sam's Club agenda aren't border-jumping migrant laborers; rather, they're second- and third-generation Americans whose interests ultimately align with the rest of the working class, white and black. That is, they're trying to move up in the world but find themselves held back—by stagnating wages, by high out-of-wedlock birth rates, by mediocre high schools and the hard road to a college degree.

These voters will be turned off by nativism, but they're unlikely to become permanently attached to a political party simply because its leadership panders on immigration and border control. And their ambitions make them naturally sympathetic to what John Fonte has termed "civic conservatism," with its emphasis on "the equality of American citizenship; the learning of America's history and values, properly understood; the imperative of assimilating immigrants patriotically into the American way of life . . . and the indivisibility of American sovereignty." Hispanics want to have their ethnic loyalties respected, but what many of them are really looking for is a party that addresses their socioeconomic concerns and respects their desire to become full-fledged Americans. Which means that conservatives can afford to speak a language of enforcement and assimilation—of increased security along the border and English in the schools—if they speak the language of working-class aspiration as well.

In the long run, the battle for the Hispanic vote won't be won along the Rio Grande, but in the debates over health care, over tax policy, over education and welfare. So instead of offering Hispanics a guest-worker plan that speaks only to their ancestral sympathies, conservatives should be offering the same opportunity agenda that they offer all Americans—health security, a family-friendly tax code, wage subsidies to help you climb out of poverty, and an educational system that lets you rise toward affluence. The ultimate goal should be a politics of solidarity, a constellation of policies that make all Americans—blacks as well as whites, the poor as well as the prosperous, recent immigrants as well as natives—believe that we're in this thing together.

9

The Frontier Society

Political parties live and die by winning elections, and in the last two chapters we presented a political program that can do just that. By making family life more secure, improving health care for all Americans, overhauling the tax code, and rebuilding the work-ethic state, conservatives can forge a lasting majority and better the lives of millions of working-class Americans. But the true test of a political movement is whether it has a long-range vision as well as a short-term agenda—one that will prepare America's families for the unfamiliar world to come.

Fortunately, many of the economic and cultural "surprises" in store for us are eminently predictable. The future is already here, in the demographics of the next generation at home and around the world. The centrist optimism of the 1990s represents one bet about this future—that globalization will benefit everyone, providing wealth enough to make up for growing insecurity, and that all we needed was to stand aside and let free trade work its magic. The more recent turn toward populism and protectionism represents another—a bet that the future for America's working class will be dark and chaotic, and that only the ultrarich will thrive as outsourcing and exotic technologies transform the world of work.

In this chapter, we will offer a bet of our own, and some policy prescriptions to go along with it. We've already seen, in Chapter 6, how global trends are threatening the prosperity of all Americans, not just the working-class voters with whom this book is particularly concerned, and how a global labor glut, in particular, threatens to make American exceptionalism a thing of the past. In this chapter, we envision an America that responds to this challenge by falling back on its inherent strengths, particularly its capacity for reinvention and renewal. Our predictions and proposals focus on efforts to open the frontier, both literally in the sense of settling and resettling America's vast interior and figuratively in the sense of extending the scope of educational freedom and civic cooperation. Some of these ideas will strike you as sober and responsible. Because this is a speculative enterprise, others will strike you as outlandish. Don't say we didn't warn you.

Wide Open Spaces

The United States has long been a frontier economy, both metaphorically and literally. We lead where others follow: When it comes to pioneering new technologies and applying them to everyday work, or finding new ways to allocate capital, Americans have tended to be first out of the gate. And we have the advantage of wide, open spaces, which enable America to periodically renew itself by turning from old, expensive, and heavily urbanized areas to literal new frontiers—whether by taking wagon trains west to Oregon and California in the nineteenth century or driving U-Hauls south to the Sun Belt in the twentieth. Indeed, America is distinctive enough that the Japanese have a word for our unique resilience, *sokojikara*. This resilience, as Joel Kotkin has observed, is built on the openness of our economy and the diversity of our population, but also on the simple fact of our sheer size.

Our geography isn't as great an advantage as it used to be, admittedly. The tremendous decrease in the cost of transporting natural resources has reduced America's advantage in resource wealth. (We buy the same oil Europeans do, for example.) Our vast internal market and common language made us unique in the nineteenth century, but modern China has similar advantages, and cheap transportation and Internet-age technology ensure that young Europeans will be able to hop around almost as much as we do and discover a common EU culture wherever they go. But all our rivals face geographical limits to growth: Japan is hedged in by mountains and the sea, and the same goes for China, while Europe is already the densest continent on earth, where cycles of urban expansion and infill have been going on for centuries and where any new growth must go upward and not outward. Not so America, which even now, more than a century after the "closing" of the frontier, enjoys the advantages of a vast, sparsely settled hinterland.

Pessimism about America's future has a natural home in the places where this size isn't in evidence—in the dense ribbon of cities that runs up and down the Atlantic and (to a lesser extent) the Pacific seaboards, where the profusion of humanity and the interminable congestion can't help but give one a gloomy outlook on twenty-first-century life. Increasingly, cities like New York represent a luxury few can afford. Here you find the personal service industries of the future, with working-class nannies and doormen bowing and scraping for the richest Americans. Or you find struggling families buying homes they can barely afford.

Such density has its benefits: Megacities like New York and Los Angeles and smaller, cosmopolitan cities like Boston and San Francisco play a critical role in a frontier economy by providing a home to the world-leading research universities that give America much of its technological edge. But while big cities are wonderful incubators for innovation, you often need a cheaper place to stretch your legs and grow. Even now, in the absence of any national pro-frontier policy, cities like Boise, Idaho, and Reno, Nevada, are filling to the brim with young people eager to make their mark far from the stratified coastal cities they're leaving behind, in areas where their wages go far further—far enough to allow for savings, to spend more time with young children, and to make starting a business an attractive proposition. These are places where Sam's Club voters are flourishing, and where cheap homes, plentiful jobs, and strong families change lives for the better and offer a model for the American future.

But while these aspirational cities are thriving, Sam's Club voters in rural America have been left behind, as the country's "micropolitan" areas are scarred by economic decline. We shouldn't be particularly concerned about these places *as* places: There's a great deal to be said for policies that focus on poor people and not poor regions, not least because regional subsidies often turn into boondoggles, with local politicians reaping most of the benefits while families struggle to get out or get by. It's easy to see efforts to save towns and counties in the northern Great Plains or Appalachia as efforts to save, well, congressional seats, even when the constituents in question would be better off elsewhere.

But what if a policy solution for rural America is tied to a solution for the costs and congestion afflicting urban America, and particularly its working-class inhabitants? In previous chapters, we discussed the problems posed by the soaring cost of living in America's biggest, densest metropolitan areas and proposed some short-term solutions. But over the long term, the most effective and lasting solution might be to pull an Abraham Lincoln: to draw on our wide, open spaces to provide new frontiers of opportunity.

The Greening of the Heartland

One way to accomplish this goal would be through a sweeping federal program. But it's worth pointing out that the northern Great Plains is already the "beneficiary" of one of the most generous federal programs of all—farm subsidies, that is. North Dakota, for example, receives approximately $9,000 per person, an amount that could, if handed out in the form of a check, lift thousands of Great Plains families out of poverty. Of course, that's not how the money is handed out—all of it goes to farm owners, people who are already ahead of the game in some respects, and a disproportionately large share goes to the biggest and the richest farmers. Instead of using the subsidies to revive rural communities, the $25 billion we spend on direct subsidies is distributed in a way that's proved positively harmful to these communities' survival, by absorbing resources that could be used elsewhere and by indirectly discouraging economic diversification. (Worse still are the subsidies for irrigation, which are so generous that farming has actually shifted *away* from well-watered regions like Iowa, where agriculture really is the first and best use for the land.) So rural America has developed the kind of economy you'd expect to find in the Third World, with farmers sticking to obsolete monocrop economies that slowly undermine the environment. You'd almost think that farm subsidies were part of a diabolical plot to drive rural families to the nearest city.

In fact, farm subsidies are a legacy of an older, more comprehensive strategy for rural America, a strategy based around providing a secure and reliable supply of food and other key resources for the urban majority. In exchange, farmers, ranchers, and other rural Americans received large subsidies to maintain a high-quality infrastructure. Once the rural population began to dwindle, though, and cheaper sources of food emerged overseas, this exchange began to be perceived, rightly, as a raw deal for urban and suburban taxpayers. As a result, farm subsidies survive only thanks to the skill and seniority of rural politicians—and the importance, every four years, of the Iowa caucuses.

Would eliminating the subsidies solve the problem of the Great Plains' economic decline? It would certainly go a long way—except that voters in the Iowa caucuses and farm-state senators are unlikely to suddenly embrace a plan that will transform, and potentially devastate, their way of life with nothing to show for it. But suppose the subsidies weren't eliminated, exactly, but instead shifted to more profitable purposes. For instance, Michael Lind has suggested that the money spent on farm subsidies could "be better used to promote a combination of service and manufacturing industries, as part of an ambitious economic-development program for the region." This would include inducements to persuade families to move westward, as well as a large-scale federal investment in high-tech infrastructure and telecommuting capacity—a twenty-first-century updating of Lincoln's transcontinental railroad or FDR's rural electrification project.

Such investments make sense, but abandoning farm subsidies entirely would involve a sweeping transformation of rural culture that's unlikely to play well with Plains State politicians. Why should farmers give up their way of life so that the government can subsidize new homes for wired telecommuters fleeing coastal crowding? Which is why it might be more politically feasible to keep farm subsidies flowing directly to farmers. But rather than paying them to grow surplus crops in semi-arid regions, we could pay them to do something that benefits the country as a whole. Like, say, cleaning up the environment.

Environmental protection isn't always the first priority of Sam's Club voters, to say the least. The language of environmentalism—particularly at the nitty-gritty level of state and local politics—often seems to privilege aesthetic concerns over the livelihood and convenience of real families. It's hardly surprising that a mother of two who saw her parents lose their mill jobs in Oakridge, Oregon, fifteen years ago doesn't have terribly warm feelings about the spotted owl. Nor should it come as a shock that a paralegal trying to find affordable housing and an easy commute in southern Connecticut would have little patience with the various strictures on building homes in "wetlands" and the not-in-my-backyard opposition to expanding I-95.

But there's a clear opportunity here for conservatives, who for too long have ceded the debate over energy independence and global warming to liberals. As the consensus surrounding the role of human-produced carbon emissions in climate change has grown stronger, conservatives have often taken a head-in-the-sand approach, which in turn has fit neatly into a larger left-wing narrative of a know-nothing, antiscience Right. Considering that American conservatives have long been identified with scientific and technological progress, this is a dangerous reversal, particularly in a fundamentally optimistic society.

As Jim Manzi has argued in the pages of *National Review*, recognizing that human-driven climate change is a real problem with the potential for sharply negative consequences doesn't mean that conservatives need to embrace liberal solutions, like the sweeping agenda proposed by former vice president Al Gore and other left-wing greens. (Newt Gingrich, hardly a devotee of fashionable liberal orthodoxies, makes a similar case in his book *A Contract with the Earth*.) Thus far, the political debate over climate change has been bizarrely one-sided, with only liberals willing to even acknowledge the facts about the issue. This has given them a free pass to propose extraordinarily expensive, intrusive, and quite possibly counterproductive measures. By absenting themselves from the field, conservatives have allowed liberals to pose as visionaries on the issue, rather than exposing them as top-down statists who are superimposing a distaste for industrial society and the suburban lifestyle on what is fundamentally a question of problem-solving.

For now, the political costs of the conservative approach have been limited, since environmentalism has been a second-order issue for most voters. But there's reason to believe that the environment will grow in political salience over time, as the impact of climate change becomes more apparent. Moreover, the debate over global warming speaks to the character of a political movement: As a rising number of conservative evangelicals have noted, the issue at stake is "creation care," the legacy we'll leave to our children, and a movement that dismisses these concerns entirely is on the fast track to self-marginalization.

Fortunately, there are species of environmentalism that are sensitive to the needs of the working class. By engaging liberals on the best approach for fighting climate change (and achieving energy independence), conservatives can make the case for an environmentalism that is pro-growth and pro-jobs. One approach, advanced by Manzi and also by reformist liberals Michael Shellenberger and Ted Nordhaus, is to eschew punitive approaches like carbon taxes or a cap-and-trade system (which is to say, a messier and more complex form of carbon taxes), and instead embrace large investments in alternative technologies, investments that can spur job creation—including "green-collar" jobs that could represent an attractive alternative for working-class Americans.

That's the idea behind ethanol subsidies, for instance, which are intended to honor the dignity of farmers by buying their products and putting them to good use, reducing our dependence on fossil fuels in the bargain. The only problem is that the current system of ethanol subsidies does very little *actual* good. Indeed, chances are that the ethanol-industrial complex is doing the opposite. Like most alternative fuels, ethanol has problems on both the demand and supply sides of the equation.

Fuels that consist primarily of ethanol—like E85, which contains only 15 percent gasoline—cost about as much as regular gas, and deliver fewer miles per gallon. If demand were high for such a fuel, there wouldn't be enough to go around. The industry is currently capable of producing about 4.8 billion gallons of ethanol a year; the United States consumes roughly 140 billion gallons of gasoline annually. As popular as ethanol is in the farm states, it's ultimately a dead end, at least until radical new technologies—like, say, an engineered bacteria that turns compost into fuel—come online.

Such technologies may be on the horizon, and they've already become a target for venture capital. If conservatives successfully make the case for an entrepreneurial approach to environmental protection, one could imagine an agency dedicated to funding alternative-energy research—modeled, perhaps, on the Defense Advanced Research Projects Agency (DARPA), which has sparked dramatic advances in the realm of defense technology. The key is to spread the money around, seeding a variety of promising projects in the hope of sparking useful innovation, rather than dumping enormous sums into a single ethanol-style Potemkin industry. There's always the risk of waste and inefficiency in any government program, but a DARPA-style approach is vastly preferable to the sort of massive, growth-killing regulatory regime promoted by the left.

So what kind of innovations might this agency promote? Among other things, it might facilitate the diffusion of flex-fuel technologies that dramatically improve fuel economy. It could encourage the decentralization of power generation and district heating, an approach that's been proven to reduce carbon emissions and enhance efficiency and that increases the resilience of our electricity grid. And it could stimulate the reform of farming practices by encouraging no-till farming and agricultural carbon sequestration.

Which brings us back to farm subsidies. Instead of paying

216

farmers to grow surplus crops, the federal government could pay them to turn biomass into charcoal, a process that removes carbon from the atmosphere and can produce a host of valuable by-products—everything from soil additives to electricity. (In theory, we could use biomass to replace nearly every other source of electricity, including dirty, polluting sources, with enough left over to power Canada.) Back in the old days, the big cities *needed* rural America for food. Right now, our cities badly need electricity—and if rural America can provide for that need, money will flow back to farms and small towns. Not only that, rural communities can capitalize on their proximity to the new black gold by diversifying their local economies, keeping families on the farm and drawing others from service-sector jobs in overpriced cities. Of course, relatively few of these folks will stick to farming. Most will flock to industries that today's entrepreneurs have barely even dreamed up.

It's true that dramatically upgrading rural America's infrastructure would make a big difference to any Great Plains renewal—whether it's the high-tech networks that Lind champions or the kind of "interstate skyway" of small airports and cheap heartland flights that James Fallows has proposed. But it's also possible that merely replacing farm subsidies with subsidies for carbon removal and other environment-friendly agricultural ventures will have an electric effect, quite literally, on rural America's economic prospects. Once we break the logjam of today's dismal nonstrategy for rural survival, we might start seeing the entrepreneurial drive that won the West in the first place—only this time the pioneers will be Sam's Club voters in minivans.

Unbundling Academia

If American life becomes more decentralized over the next half century, American education will need to follow suit. We've already discussed the weaknesses of the current higher education system, in which colleges—private and public alike—compete to attract the narrow demographic of upper-middle-class students whose tuition dollars boost endowments and whose average SAT score raises a school's *U.S. News & World Report* rankings. This has led to slow-motion stratification, by throwing up barriers to working-class students; at the same time, it has led our country to overvalue a four-year, on-campus college education and shortchange the kind of vocational and technical training that might benefit people from all social classes.

There are a number of small-bore ways to improve this picture. Class-based affirmative action is one obvious (and popular) option; another would be to shift public funding around to reward public colleges that graduate larger numbers of low-income students and cut funds to those that don't; still another would be to simply slash funding for flagship state universities, which are capable of fending (and fund-raising) for themselves, and hike spending for regional public institutions and community colleges, which are more likely to enroll students from working-class backgrounds. State governments might also consider offering bonuses to schools that boost their graduation rates, as New York State recently began to do—since one of the things that keep young people in the working class from moving up isn't their failure to enter college but their likelihood of dropping out.

But in the long run, we should be looking to more radical approaches. For instance, state governments might ask how well they are serving their constituents by funding public universities directly and relying on the schools to disburse the funds as they see fit. If the point of a public university is to hire superstar faculty, build amazing research facilities, and compete with Harvard or Yale, then perhaps this kind of funding makes sense. But if the point of spending public money is to further the public's access to education, then it might be worth considering alternative means of pursuing those ends.

With this in mind, Ohio University economist Richard Vedder has suggested that states start offering education money directly to prospective students in the form of tuition vouchers, redeemable at any state institution. These could be staggered according to financial need: If the average tuition in a state university system is $10,000, a poor student might receive a voucher for $9,000 and a wealthy student a voucher for $4,000. In this landscape, schools would have an obvious financial incentive to admit a balance of rich and lower-income undergraduates. The upper-class students would do more to raise the school's average SAT score and alumni giving, but the poorer students would bring in more tuition dollars. Like the Summer Opportunity Scholarships we discussed in the previous chapter, such a program might be able to command support from both sides of the political aisle: The system's market-based efficiency would delight free marketeers, while its potential for boosting access might win the support of egalitarian-minded liberals. And a vouchered approach to funding state schools could go hand in hand with reduced state oversight of higher education, which would please academics and administrators tired of having cost-conscious legislators looking over their shoulders.

Such decentralization is on its way in any case. Consider the example of for-profit universities, which increasingly cater to working-class students looking to get credentialed without shelling out their valuable time and money for a four-year degree. Unregulated and driven by bottom-line concerns, these schools often enroll students who can't do the work or promise job opportunities that never materialize. But they tend to serve exactly the kind of student that meritocracy leaves behind, and do so at a fraction of the cost of traditional colleges. Much of this success derives from for-profit schools' ability to "unbundle" a college education from its traditional (and costly) campus environment—an unbundling made possible in large part by the spread of the Internet. Some for-profit schools are entirely Web based, and many others rely on online libraries, class registration, and even advising. This is obviously not a model that a flagship state university is likely to follow anytime soon, but even in the Ivy League, parts of the academic environment are relocating into cyberspace. As Charles Murray points out, "These and other developments are all still near the bottom of steep growth curves. The cost of effective training will fall for everyone who is willing to give up the trappings of a campus. As the cost of college continues to rise, the choice to give up those trappings will become easier."

It's true that the more market efficiency you inject into higher education, and the more you emphasize practical training over the traditional academic experience, the more the liberal arts would be likely to suffer. Computing classes would crowd out Shakespeare; management courses would replace musical instruction; everyone would learn Spanish and no one Latin. But for Americans trying to compete in a global economy, it's the computer courses and the Spanish lessons that matter, and the career-enhancing credential that comes with them. Students are already voting with their feet and their tuition dollars. As two college presidents recently pointed out, the nation's "liberal arts college students would almost certainly fit easily inside a Big Ten football stadium: fewer than 100,000 students out of more than 14 million." Liberal arts education is already the preserve of the very few, and in a country where a third of American undergrads work full-time and over half attend school part-time, it seems perverse to insist that our system cater more to the needs of the upper-middle class than to the many.

If we really want an educational system that serves the interests of the working class, though, the long-term goal should be to roll back our current credentialing regime completely. Most Americans who seek out college degrees do so because it's the best way to signal to prospective employers that they have the skills the company is looking for. But making credentialing dependent on four years of college sets the barriers to entry so high that it limits competition and shuts out ambitious Americans who lack the time and money to acquire a four-year degree. And employers lose out, too, since at best, looking at an applicant's college transcript offers an indirect sense of his potential competence. (As Walter Russell Mead points out, "It is the easiest thing in the world today to find English majors with B.A. degrees from accredited colleges who cannot write a standard business letter.")

A far fairer system would assign credentials on the basis of examinations, either national or state-level, that evaluate students on the basis of the actual skills they'll need to do their jobs well. The results of the exams would be available to any employer who accessed a national database. A person could take the same exam more than once to demonstrate increased proficiency. Exams of a similar nature could be used to supplement or even replace a traditional college education. Abraham Lincoln proved to be a pretty successful lawyer despite never having attended an accredited law school. It's only fair that we give today's young people the same opportunity.

New Kinds of Education

The goal of all these reforms would be to take the logic of the elite workplace, where learning is continuous and work is supposed to be engaging rather than arduous, and apply it to the population as a whole. One of the most tragic inequalities in American life today is the way that fulfilling work—work that resembles mind-expanding play more than the daily grind—is limited to a happy few. The dignity we associate with the skilled trades and farming, jobs where hardworking individuals are owners and producers, not just employees, is hard to find among the non–college-educated. Restoring dignity to work has to be an essential part of a long-term Sam's Club agenda, and embracing robust experimentation in education is a necessary first step.

Consider two examples of where such experimentation might lead. The first is toward a greater emphasis on teaching craftsmanship, whether it takes the form of high-school shop classes or advances in computer simulation that enable would-be craftsmen to train themselves online. One consequence of the growth of America's mass upper class has been an explosion of demand for highly skilled manual laborers, from carpenters and painters to masons and electricians—a demand that far outpaces supply, as anyone who has tried to hire a landscaper or remodel a home can attest. It helps that you can't outsource plumbing or glazing or auto repair. As Matthew Crawford, a scholar and motorcycle repairman, notes in the *New Atlantis*, "While manufacturing jobs have certainly left our shores to a disturbing degree, the manual trades have not. If you need a deck built, or your car fixed, the Chinese are of no help. Because they are in China."

These are jobs that don't require a college degree, or any degree at all, for that matter, and they pay extremely well: A journeyman craftsman can expect to enjoy an above-average income; master craftsmen routinely earn in the low six figures. They provide work that's in demand in cities and suburbs, exurbs and rural counties—wherever there are decks to be built, apartments to be wired, and pipes to be welded. And they offer an antidote to the deadening effects of too many modern jobs, both blue and white collar. As Crawford puts it, the "physical circumstances of the jobs performed by carpenters, plumbers, and auto mechanics vary too much for them to be executed by idiots; they require circumspection and adaptability. One feels like a man, not a cog in a machine."

At present, there's an aversion to teaching these trades in public schools. Crawford writes that the "egalitarian worry that has always attended tracking students into 'college prep' and 'vocational ed' is overlaid with another: the fear that acquiring a specific skill set means that one's life is determined." But in the age of the global labor glut, the opposite may be the case. The twentysomething with a generic college degree and no particular skill set could actually have fewer options than the twentysomething who knows how to landscape a yard or paint a house. Similarly, a laid-off autoworker in Michigan might be better off getting retrained as a mechanic or an electrician than as an office worker with a data entry job that could easily be outsourced to Bangalore.

If experimentation in education can expand our definition of a "student" to include a laid-off autoworker learning carpentry on weekends or online, it might expand our definition of what constitutes a "teacher" as well. In Chapter 8, we discussed a possible education reform, the weighted student formula, that would allow for choice and competition within the boundaries of school districts. But for parents in the (hopefully reviving) expanse of rural America, chances are there won't be enough students to sustain a large number of local schools or the kind of intradistrict competition that produces significant results. In an age of growing telecommuting, it's likely that some combination of distance education and homeschooling will offer an increasingly attractive alternative to the local public school—which will mean that more and more parents will double as part-time teachers.

In 1980, roughly 50,000 children were educated at home, mostly by hippie parents who had tuned in and dropped out of the Man's public school system. By 2003, the National Center for Education Statistics estimated that 1.1 million students were being homeschooled; homeschooling advocates place the figure at closer to 2 million. (By way of comparison, an estimated

700,000 students are currently enrolled in charter schools.) Evangelical Christians led the way, but as Brian Anderson of the Manhattan Institute pointed out in 2000, the "full array of American families—from religiously orthodox Catholics and Jews to thoroughgoing secularists—are joining the fundamentalists and the Age-of-Aquarius types in home schooling their kids." It's a phenomenon that crosses lines of race and class as well. Fifteen percent of homeschooling parents are black and Hispanic, half of homeschooling families have incomes of $50,000 or less, and three-quarters earn $75,000 or less. "The rise of home schooling," Patricia Lines wrote in the *Public Interest* in 2000, "is one of the most significant social trends of the past half century."

Right now, though, homeschooling families are caught in a bind. Sacrificing parental income is perhaps the most obvious cost, but there's also the inefficiency of having a father who has mastered the art of teaching fourth-grade math move on to fifth-grade history while never using those skills he's acquired ever again. As homeschooling continues to expand, this waste of skill and experience will grow ever larger. Meanwhile, thousands of children who could draw on a homeschooling parent's expertise are at the mercy of substandard schools.

One obvious solution would be for state and local regulators to encourage the formation of large-scale cooperative networks that can marry adults with the ability to teach with children with a need to learn. Drawing on the experience of an entire community means that these open schools will offer the kind of knowledge base even the most innovative principals can't imagine drawing on. Eventually these networks could expand from underserved communities to all parts of the country. And they wouldn't need to include only parents. A pharmacist could supplement his income by teaching high-school-level chemistry a few hours a week, an accountant could double as a part-time math teacher—and a carpenter or welder could run shop classes out of his workshop. The very nature of this system, if you can even call it that, will likely prove so decentralized and so responsive to changing demand that it will pioneer entirely new fields of education.

Workers of the World

This kind of community-based education depends on flourishing communities—families that look out for other families and neighborhoods that buzz with life. As we saw in Chapter 7, "sprawl" has actually *increased* social interaction, whether we're talking about personal friendships or the propensity to join civic and religious organizations. It's true that Americans rely more on their immediate families for emotional support than has traditionally been the case. But many technological advances are working with, rather than against, those who hope to increase the level of civic cooperation. Indeed, the last decade has as a result seen a largely unheralded renaissance in civic life, reflected in everything from the rise of Internet communities to the proliferation of coffee shops.

But this renaissance has yet to reach the workplace. In 1955, the golden age of organized labor, 37 percent of private-sector workers belonged to a union. Fifty years later, that number has fallen to 7.9 percent. The collapse of organized labor leaves a real vacuum: Where do American workers turn when they face serious problems at the office or on the shop floor? Short of quitting, what can you do to make a difference in your working life, for most people one of the most important commitments they have? We can, of course, hope and expect that every employer will be benevolent and do everything possible to look after their employees, but inevitably, many companies fall short of this lofty ideal. That's part of the reason the American left is taking a second look at old-school unions. Open the pages of the *American Prospect* or the *Nation* and you'll find renewed excitement about organizing drives and about legislation designed to help unions expand.

But chances are, such old-school unionism will never make a comeback. Union density in America won't magically increase to European levels, or to 1955 levels for that matter, and as long as that's the case, unionized firms will have significantly higher costs than their nonunion counterparts. Consider the fate of Detroit's dying automobile industry and you'll see why an employer doesn't need to be a dastardly moustache-twirler to entertain doubts about the effect unionization will have on the bottom line. For similar reasons, rank-and-file workers don't always need management to convince them that joining a union could mean declining profits and lost jobs. Liberals are pressing for "card check," for instance, which would allow union certification as soon as a majority of workers in a company declared their support—that is, it would get rid of secret ballots for union drives. The idea is that employers would have a tougher time intimidating workers out of backing unions. There's no doubt that some employers really do pressure the rank and file. But the truth is that many workers really are choosing not to join unions. The last comprehensive study of worker preferences, from the late 1990s, found that 32 percent of nonunion employees in the private sector want unions. While that's nothing to scoff at, the pro-union constituency represents a distinct minority.

If workplace organization has a future, it will need to adapt to the demands of a more competitive and volatile era. The first and most obvious step to take is to reform our labor laws. According to Harvard labor economist Richard Freeman, large numbers of American workers—78 percent in the survey cited above—are more receptive to staff associations and other nonunion forms of worker representation. These are elected groups that bring grievances to management on issues ranging from wages to hours to serious harassment and abuse. Such nonunion groups are less confrontational than unions, but more effective than relying solely on the goodwill of management when it comes to solving workplace problems. The trouble is, staff associations, or "company unions," are banned under the National Labor Relations Act. If the vast majority of workers who choose not to join a union are ever going to have a voice in their companies, this has to change.

Staff associations can go only so far. Like unions, they're tied to a workplace, not to individuals. A staff association can make a particular job more tolerable, but that's about it. Fortunately, a new model of unionism is slowly emerging, one that focuses on providing tangible benefits that follow workers from job to job, rather than negotiating ironclad contracts that last a lifetime. The same technology-enabled cooperation that's reviving America's neighborhoods just might provide a road back to prominence for what was once a mainstay of working-class life in America.

The Freelancers Union, for instance, founded in the 1990s, now provides a basic health-care plan to thousands of New Yorkers who offer contract labor—doing everything from freelance writing to tech support—and the group is planning to expand its offerings to include a retirement plan. Whereas traditional labor unions tend to have adversarial relationships with management, fighting for benefits tooth and nail, new model unions could make management almost superfluous: Like the old "friendly societies" of prewar Britain, they could draw on the resources of their members to create cooperative solutions to problems ranging from health care to pensions. Management would pay their salaries, but would be in a sense incidental to an economic arrangement that focuses on serving the needs of individual workers.

It's easy to see how far this model could go, given half a chance. What if unions focused primarily on making their members hot commodities rather than long-term obligations? In Las Vegas, the city described by some unionists as the "postindustrial De-troit," service sector unions have focused on teaching immigrant workers English and providing them with the skills they need to steadily move up the occupational ladder, rather than trying to keep them frozen in a specific job, or industry, throughout their entire career. Las Vegas's unique environment is difficult to rep-licate elsewhere, and yet this basic idea, of unions as learning organizations that offer crucial support systems to workers in a variety of industries, hits the right note.

In the long run, unions might evolve into enormous talent agencies with an economic stake in increasing the wages of members by, for example, taking some small cut of any salary increase and then reinvesting the money into providing work-ers with the resources to move from sluggish labor markets to booming labor markets. Whereas traditional unions have an interest in keeping workers in one place, new model unions would encourage them to be footloose, all while maintaining strong ties to their fellow workers. Corporations would eventu-ally turn to the best-managed unions to meet staffing needs.

The most powerful trend in industrial organization is toward the steady disaggregation of vertically integrated corporations into what some scholars call open process networks. Apart from core business functions, virtually everything a modern busi-ness does can be farmed out to other specialized firms—and in-deed, to specialized individuals—who can do the job better and cheaper. (One harbinger of the future is eBay's new program that provides discounts for health insurance to the "PowerSell-ers" who generate the most revenue for the company.)

Assuming this trend continues, new model unions could very well displace for-profit corporations as the dominant entities in the economy, thanks to their loyal pools of talent. Naturally, some companies will try to beat them at their own game—which is why these unions will have to work hard to earn the loyalty and trust of their members. Either way, workers win.

The Promise of American Life

What all of these ideas, from the sober to the speculative, have in common is a vision of working-class independence—from bosses, from bureaucracy, from entrenched interests of all kinds. This is what the next working-class majority needs to provide—a government that offers basic institutional support, whether you're raising a child or caring for a sick relative or trying to carve out a fulfilling working life, but that always treats you as a free individual rather than client, a citizen rather than a subject. It should be a government that supports innovators and self-starters of all stripes, and always takes the side of the common man rather than a narrow, credentialed elite.

The New Deal–era reformers, whose story we began with, saw the advent of a new technological era as a threat to the dignity and independence of the American family and strove to protect a form of democratic self-reliance within a stratified industrial order. They succeeded, in large part, but the result was a prosperous working class whose independence depended on the benevolence of powerful and remote institutions—big business, big labor, and big government. And their majority broke apart, in the end, because it was *too* collectivist: Its iron triangle strangled entrepreneurial freedom, its conformism stifled cultural creativity, its racial and sexual restrictions prevented millions of Americans from realizing their full potential. Whereas today, by contrast, technological change offers not only a multitude of risks to the American way of life, but also a chance, if we can seize it, to recapture some of the bracing independence of America's earliest days.

The promise of American life, Crèvecoeur wrote in 1784, in his famous *Letters from an American Farmer*, isn't necessarily great wealth but rather "ample subsistence," and a society in which every citizen is "animated with the spirit of an industry which is unfettered and unrestrained, because each person works for himself . . . without any part being claimed, either by a despotic prince, a rich abbot, or a mighty lord." This has always been the defining feature of our national life, the root of our exceptionalism, and the secret of our success. It's the only American dream worth pursuing, because in pursuing it, we will remain as we began—a society of free men, equal in our independence, and co-owners of this almost–Promised Land.

ACKNOWLEDGMENTS

At a barbecue held just outside the Beltway around the time we embarked on this project, a noted movie critic told one of us that coauthorship is fatal to any friendship—resentments build and smolder until minor differences in "work styles" seem like grounds for murder. There were times in the following year when we understood what he meant, but we're pleased to report that our friendship survived the writing of this book—not least, we suspect, because it was the ideas contained in these pages that brought us together in the first place. Our becoming friends was facilitated by the great Steven Menashi, but it was cemented by the fact that we found ourselves agreeing quite a lot; indeed, we practically finished each other's thoughts, which was a bit eerie given that we are as different as two middle-class American nerds born a month apart can possibly be. (Check the jacket photo if you must.)

Back in 2004, when we first started discussing this project, our shared belief that the GOP was headed for rocky shoals wasn't exactly all the rage. So when one of us decided to write a short opinion piece on "The Crisis of 'Sam's Club' Republicans," the other was there to offer intellectual ammo, to sharpen the argument, and to polish the prose. You might say we were coauthors even before we were coauthors. It was only natural that we teamed up to write the article "The Party of Sam's Club," which turned into the book you are reading right now. But even two writers can't produce a book without a little (or more than a little) help from their friends, so we would like to begin by thanking David Brooks—for his advice and encouragement, and for serving as a model of the kind of public intellectual we'd both like to be: smart, judicious, generous to his detractors, and unfailingly kind. (Also, on a less prosaic note, we thank him for having given one of us a job. Without David, this book would never exist, and one of us would likely be eking out a meager living harvesting electronic gold in *World of Warcraft*.)

Bill Kristol, Richard Starr, and Matt Continetti of the *Weekly Standard* very generously gave us a chance to work out our oddball ideas at great length. Adam Bellow thought our *Standard* piece had the makings of a book, and we are grateful for his editorial guidance, and grateful to our agent, Rafe Sagalyn, for making everything possible. Jesse Shapiro, a great mind of our generation and a dear friend, pored over our harebrained schemes to separate the *halal* from the *haram*. We can't say he didn't warn us. Jonathan Chait, a friend and mentor, and Ruy Teixeira, one of the political minds we admire most, provided early insights and advice. Nick Goldberg got the ball rolling at the *Los Angeles Times*. Both Brink Lindsey and Tyler Cowen will find much to disagree with in these pages, but they nevertheless saved us from all manner of errors and from some lazy reasoning. Ramesh Ponnuru provided moral support and a wealth of sharp ideas. Andrew Sullivan has been a mentor and friend to both of us throughout the writing process and before.

As you may have noticed, this book is about the future of the Republican Party. Because we both grew up in the heart of Blue America, however, it's also a mash note to hardworking friends, teachers, and relatives who would never even dream of voting Republican. (Not yet, at least.)

And it's also a tribute to comrades of all political persuasions, from paleocons to neocons to theocons to neolibs to social democrats to reformed Sandinistas to . . . basically to all our friends and colleagues who share our belief that all is not well with American democracy, and that we as citizens have a responsibility to do something about it. Thanks to everyone we've argued with, mostly with affection and good humor—especially David Adesnik, Michael Barbaro, James Bennet, Elana Berkowitz, Julie Bosman, David Bradley, Jeremy Bronson, Chris Brose, Katie Burch, James Carmichael, Josh Chafetz, Conor Clarke, Elbridge Colby, Matt Crawford, Michael Crowley, Rebecca Dana, Mauro De Lorenzo, Rachel Dry, Susan Ellingwood, Matt Feeney, Boris Fishman, Rachel Friedman, Dan Fruchter, Anna Galland, James Gibney, Jonah Goldberg, Michael Goldfarb, Stephen Goldsmith, Erica Grieder, Toby Harshaw, Bill Hatfield, Chris Hayes, Ben Healy, Kerry Howley, Hua Hsu, Lindsay Jones, Richard Just, Anya Kamenetz, Razib Khan, Mark Kirby, Ezra Klein, Joel Kotkin, Sana Krasikov, Dan Kurtz-Phelan, Daniel Larison, Josh Levin, Yuval Levin, Min Lieskovsky, Tod Lindberg, Ryan Lizza, Christian Lorentzen, John Mangin, Katherine Mangu-Ward, Jim Manzi, Chris Matthews, Cary McClelland, Carmel McCoubrey, Ben McKean, Gabriel Mendlow, Cheryl Miller, Siddharth Mohandas, Jason Moring, Justin Muzinich, Nancy Nathan, Chris Papagianis, Chris Park, Nick Parrillo, Sasha Polakow-Suransky, Matt Quirk, Jeremy Reff, Ben Rhodes, Campbell Robertson, James Ryerson, Kareem Saleh, Will Saletan, Noam Scheiber, Laura Secor, Vance Serchuk, David Shipley, Jaime Sneider, Rich So, Ben Soskis, Peter Suderman, Chris Suellentrop, Kate Taylor, Victoria Thompson, Ben Wallace-Wells, Ben Wikler, Will Wilkinson, Rosten Woo, Graeme Wood, Richard Yeselson, and last but not least Matthew Yglesias.

And finally, Abby, whose brilliant edits improved this book immeasurably—and who was foolhardy enough to agree to marry one of us even *after* reading it.

INDEX

235

ABOUT THE AUTHORS

ROSS DOUTHAT is the author of *Privilege: Harvard and the Education of the Ruling Class* and an associate editor at the *Atlantic*. He is the film critic for *National Review*, and he blogs at rossdouthat.theatlantic.com. He lives with his wife in Baltimore, Maryland.

REIHAN SALAM is an associate editor at the *Atlantic*. He lives in Washington, D.C.